METAPHYSICAL DIVINE WISDOM

on Psychic Spirit Team Heaven Communication

A Practical Motivational Guide to Spirituality Series

KEVIN HUNTER

WARRIOR
OF LIGHT
PRESS

Warrior of Light Press
www.kevin-hunter.com

First Edition: July 2019
Printed in the United States of America

All rights reserved. Copyright © 2019
ISBN-13: 978-1733196208

3. Mind and Body. 2. Spirituality. 1. Title

DEDICATION

For you on your soul's spiritual journey.

METAPHYSICAL DIVINE WISDOM
BOOK SERIES

On Psychic Spirit Team Heaven Communication
On Soul Consciousness and Purpose
On Increasing Prayer with Faith for an Abundant Life
On Balancing the Mind, Body, and Soul
On Manifesting Fearless Assertive Confidence
On Universal, Physical, Spiritual and Soul Love

♥

Contents

>>※«•»※«•»※«•»※«•»※«•»※«•»※«•

AUTHOR NOTE

The *Metaphysical Divine Wisdom* books are a series of spiritually based books that focus on different areas of one's life. Like many of my spiritual related metaphysical books, this one is also infused with practical messages and spirit guidance that my Spirit team has taught and shared with me revolving around many different topics. The main goal is to fine-tune your body, mind, and soul. Like all souls, you are a Divine communicator capable of receiving messages and guidance from Heaven.

My personal Spirit team council makes up God and the Holy Spirit, as well as a team of guides, angels, and sometimes Archangels and Saints. I am merely the liaison or messenger in delivering and interpreting the intentions of what they wish to communicate. My team comprises some hard truth telling Wise Ones from the Other Side, including Saint Nathaniel, who can be brutal in his direct forcefulness. He cuts right to the heart of humanity without apology. I have learned quite a bit from him while adopting his ideology, which is Heaven's philosophy. I wouldn't preach Divine Guidance that God doesn't whisper into my Clairaudient ear first.

If I use the word "He" when pertaining to God, this does not mean that I am advocating that he is a male. Simply replace the word, "He" with one you are comfortable using to identify God for you to be. If the word, "God" makes you uncomfortable, then substitute it with one you're more accustomed with like Universe, Spirit, Energy, the Light, or any other comparable word. This goes for any gender I use as examples. When I say, "spirit team", I am referring to a team of 'Guides and Angels'.

One of the purposes of my work is to empower, enlighten, as well as entertain. It's also to help you improve yourself, your soul, your life and humanity by default. If anything, I am preaching to myself, because God knows that I can use a refresher course occasionally. It does not matter if you are a beginner or well versed in the subject matter. There may be something that reminds you of something you already know or something that you were unaware of. We all have much to share with one another, as we are all one in the end.

~ Kevin Hunter

METAPHYSICAL DIVINE WISDOM

ON PSYCHIC SPIRIT TEAM
HEAVEN COMMUNICATION

CHAPTER ONE

*I Am Psychic
and So Are You!*

Connecting with my Divine Spirit team through channeling sometimes requires taking a deep breath in if I'm not relaxed followed by shutting my eyes on the exhale. The second my eyes close, the connection with spirit is dramatically established as if pushing an electrical plug into a wall socket that creates a spark. The initial connection entails being immediately catapulted through the air like a cannonball firing. It can move in numerous ways where I'm soaring at lightning speed through the vortex portal of the next plane only to slam into an ocean plummeting downwards deeper and faster into its dark watery depths that accelerates in a fashion comparable to a rocket gaining steam, then the messages float into my consciousness.

One of the other ways is the missile firing is followed by a bomb explosion going off leaving me surrounded by brilliant shining bright white light. This is only to realize I've been moving at rapid speed within it. The light breaks apart and dissolves into billions of stars. This interstellar display evaporates, and the laws of human physics are defied as I ascend higher by means of what some call astral travel and projection. This intergalactic travelling through light years of galaxy and space is where the messages sift into my consciousness.

I have no idea where I'll be taken until I shut my eyes only to discover my vessel is travelling upwards or downwards. The chilling transporting happens if I'm sent into the depths of the ocean, as there is a few second shock and fear of potential drowning. This is followed by a heaviness that luckily subsides into contentment the further I plunge into its intense profoundness. Crossing into the portal I'm surrounded by members of my Spirit council in a comfortable gigantic wave of strengthening love like being hugged to death. Everything grows exceedingly calm while in this brilliant transcending radiance.

This way of communication isn't unusual for me as I've been a natural born psychic since childhood. One of the greater misunderstandings about psychic phenomena is that only a select group of people on the planet are gifted with psychic perception. Because of that belief some have either lifted psychics into special royalty status or discredited psychic foresight altogether. I am psychic and so are you! Every living-breathing organism is psychic from people, to plants, to animals, and to the entire planet. Everything that is not human made but God created has access to these Divine communication receptors deep within the soul's DNA, regardless if there is awareness of that or not. This is one of the ways that everything and everyone is affected and connected to one another.

When you walk into a room full of people and someone is angry and creating a dramatic scene, then every single person in that room will be negatively affected by it. I've been in restaurants where someone nearby our table has this infectious hysterical laugh that makes us, and the surrounding tables light up in laughter as well too. When I was working on {a film production for Warner Bros. Studios} *The Perfect Storm*, I had answered my phone and it was one of the Assistant Directors calling from the soundstage. He paused moving from serious and formal to lightening and warming up to tell me, "You know Kevin, I could be having the most stressful day on set, but as soon as you answer the phone there is this sudden calmness that relaxes me. It's every single time that sometimes I'll admit I'm not calling you for anything important, but I just need to absorb some of what is coming off you. I spoke to others on set about it and they all agreed and said they had noticed the same thing too."

Back during those entertainment day job days,

my boss wouldn't always take his car to work and would be driven or use other transportation because it was less stressful. I said to him once, "I live past you now, so if there are ever days you want to ride let me know. I don't mind I like the company."

There were days that he started to take me up on that offer. As months passed by, I ran into his husband who said to me, "I can tell the days that he rides home with you. Because those are the only days that he comes home calm, relaxed, and in good spirits."

The psychic energy that people give off and radiate transfers to other people in the vicinity. When you're radiating a serene, loving, calmness, then those around can feel and absorb that. When you have a terribly toxic roommate, friend, colleague, spouse, or family member, everyone notices it and is negatively affected that it can ruin their day. These emotions that cause others to detect, pick up on, and absorb those other energies off other people is connected to your Clairsentience psychic feeling sense. It acts like a suction cup that breathes in everything that is around it both the good and the bad from the physical, supernatural and ethereal.

Your aura is six feet in all directions around your body. This is how big every human soul's light is. If someone's auric circle is plagued with Darkness and they walk past you, then it will hit your auric circle. This is how it affects your well-being state and vice versa since everything is made of energy. If you read toxic media, news, or social media that upsets you, then the energy of that news and the person that wrote it is emanating off that and hitting your aura. This is all part of another handful of reasons as to why it's important to protect your soul's Light and sensitivities. This means getting strict and disciplined by what you allow close to your auric circle. You're doing that to protect you and your soul from unnecessary dark energies that offer no positive benefit at all. By doing this you are managing your souls light the same way you manage other areas of your life from work, home, to relationships. Often neglected and forgot about is the soul's spiritual life, which is affected by everything around it. It's the same way someone taps on an Aquarium glass where a fish is sitting prompting it to dart away.

With Clairsentience you can walk into a place and sense a dark gloom, which is a psychic signal to high tail it out of there. The feelings people have are one of the most powerful ways that psychic information comes in, but when you're so focused on your feelings and how you feel, then you don't realize that sometimes it's a psychic hit coming through from spirit. This is the case until you learn through repetitive practice how to recognize when it's a psychic hit or your ego mind.

It is true that some people tend to display stronger psychic senses than others, but that doesn't mean other people don't have those same psychic senses. The more blocked someone is, then the more reduced those psychic senses are to the extent that it would appear they have no psychic abilities at all. Those psychic abilities are buried deep down in that soul without them realizing it.

There are endless lists of things that can block someone from noticing Divine psychic guidance. The saying that states you are what you eat or drink is true. The foods you consume can create a psychic block with the Divine. The more bad foods you consume, then the dimmer the psychic senses will be. Altering your state of mind through drugs and alcohol will dim your psychic senses. This isn't scolding anyone or instructing anyone not to have those comfort foods like that hot dog at an amusement park or a glass of wine with a lover. This is informing you what can reduce or dim your psychic abilities. The good news is that you can have that day of fun where your psychic senses have been dimmed, but then it's assumed it's not like you're doing that every day. The next day you may then choose to get re-aligned and healthy again. Consuming toxins daily if you're unable to stop should be reduced to moderation beyond enhancing your psychic abilities. It is also less taxing on your body in the long run as your medical doctor may at some point advise you if they haven't already. Believe me I still love my Classic Rock music blaring at a Beach BBQ with a cold beer in my hand, but I know in that moment my psychic prowess is dimming. I can hear my Spirit team council, but they're distant as if talking through a wall separating us.

Negative emotions of any kind will dim psychic clair senses. This includes any negative emotion you can possibly think of from anger, stress, depression, sadness, grief, agitation, frustration, vindictiveness, greed, and gossip and on and on. I know we basically listed most of the generic negative emotional traits that all human beings experience at one time or another, with some displaying those traits more than others. This isn't telling anyone to deny those emotions, because you will feel them just as the highest holy person will in their own way on occasion. We are all having a human experience and with that come those challenging emotions, but that is one of the reasons why we are having a human experience. It is to be able to learn how to master our emotions and thoughts as much as possible through spiritual maturity. You're allowed to have an off day. This is encouraged as it gets you through the transformation process of hitting the floor and learning how to rebuild yourself back up. You can have numerous off days. The more you work on evolving your soul and physical experience, then the easier it gets in moving yourself right back into faith and centered in the Light when you step off balance.

When someone is twenty years old they may overreact emotionally to every little thing, but by the time they're forty years old, one hopes through the challenging life experiences thrown at them and through spiritual maturity they have grown quite good at re-centering themselves after a bad couple of days. Life experiences will throw you a hard-fisted right to the face. Many human beings will or have experienced a job loss that causes worry, depression, and fear. People have lovers that leave them causing anger, upset, and sadness. Human beings also experience the loss of loved ones, which can produce heavy grief and crushing despair. These are all part of the emotions associated with human life. You feel those emotions and you process them on your own time.

Eventually on your trajectory of soul evolvement you reach a point where you grow exhausted from feeling like that and you begin the process of taking steps to alter that into faith, hope, and action. This can be from reaching out to others for assistance, support, to changing your diet, exercising regularly, to learning to walk away from toxic people and choices. To re-align your psychic soul vessel, you might choose to listen to inspiring music, go into nature to hang out and commune, or read self-help books that can motivate you to feel joy and serenity again. You can also do what I do which is to access God and my Spirit team from within the core being of my soul. This is where I ask them through prayer to empower me all over again by lifting me right back up into warrior mode ready to conquer the world and forge forward fearlessly. I know that I cannot sit around waiting to die or feeling the same negative emotions day after day with no end in sight. I must rise back up and get back out there.

An ex once said, "The great thing that you do is you rarely get angry, but when you do everyone scatters and we all know it's serious and no drill. But you leave and come back fifteen minutes later and you're all smiles and have got over it. You don't hold onto it for any longer. Most people hang onto it forever never letting it go."

I said, "How dreadful to hold onto that forever."

Many want the rewards without doing the work. This goes for psychic development as well too. Those that have taken an interest in psychic development want the psychic prowess, but will find the development to opening the psychic senses to be dull work. If you want any reward, then you must do the work and continue to be controlled about it. There is no way around that, but if you want something bad enough, then you will work hard to achieve it through regular discipline and hard work. When you exercise regularly, you are building up stamina and toning your body. This is the same way you regularly partake in spiritual pursuits to strengthen the psychic soul part of you.

The soul in the human body is psychic, but the physical body is not psychic, yet both the spiritual body and the physical body work in tandem with one another while on Earth. Working on both helps ensure the other is working at optimum levels. When you work on your physical body by being mindful of what you are doing to it, then this simultaneously strengthens the spiritual body, which brings out those psychic senses. Strengthening your spiritual body can simultaneously strengthen your physical body. Therefore, taking care of both and keeping them at optimum levels is beneficial on your overall well-being for a variety of reasons. One is that it gives you stronger psychic Clair sense channels that guide you along your life's path helping you make better decisions. Another is that it keeps you physically healthy for as long as possible while you are here.

This gives you more energy and focus to dive into your passions and life purpose, as well as fun time with loved ones, friends, and family.

Watch what you ingest each day making sure the ratio from healthy to unhealthy shows the healthy being in a higher percentage while allowing yourself the fun you want to do. Physical exercise has been one of the top things that Spirit showed me since childhood to be of importance. I subconsciously knew as an eight-year-old that we have to take care of our bodies. Often there's a disconnect between the body and the soul, but while here they need to work in tandem since they both positively feed off of and work for one another. When you're feeling negative emotions, then this affects your physical body, which transfers to affecting your etheric psychic senses.

Physical exercise would not apply to someone that is physically unable to due to a health issue. This is more for those that don't want to out of laziness or procrastination. I've always been into physical fitness. It started at the early age of five teaching myself to ride a bike on my own, which naturally I fell a number of times, then ran into a cactus on another and created a tiny scar that's still there, but eventually I mastered it and got it going and have continued the exercise routines since. I never looked at it as work, but have always just enjoyed being active. Decades later and my disciplined exercise routine has yet to permanently stop. Even during my heavy alcohol and drug addicted days I was still managing to incorporate some exercise on certain days. The stronger your body is made through exercise, then the stronger your psychic channel is. One of my Medium friends rides her bike daily in between reading sessions for clients. She'll also treat herself to the occasional beer. You'll note the balance between the working on our physical body through exercise, but allowing yourself that toxin once in a while if you choose. Although having one beer is much different than drinking a six pack regularly.

Your emotional state is as important as your physical body, both of which also work off each other. When you exercise there has been long running scientific evidence that it positively improves your emotional state and well-being. You're improving two things at the same time by doing one thing. That one thing is the exercise that kills two birds with one stone by improving your physical health state and simultaneously your emotional and mental state. There might be a day where I fall into a slump, but then I exercise and hop on the bike and hit the beach. When I arrive back home, I feel rejuvenated and uplifted. I've walked into the gym moody and distant, but then after almost an hour of listening to music and working on the weight machines I've found all of that has shifted. Suddenly I walk out smiling with this uplifting joyful feeling like I'm on top of the world. This is because exercise also helps in raising the feel-good Dopamine chemicals in the body.

Those two examples included additional tips that raise your vibration level. When you raise your soul's vibration, then the more enhanced your psychic channels get. The biking (exercise) on the beach (nature) is a winning combo because you're uniting two elements that help raise your vibration. You're combining exercise with nature. Getting out into a nature setting has many positive benefits on both your spiritual body and emotional body.

Nature has been another scientific proven method that has been shown to reduce stress levels in people. When you reduce stress and move into a relaxation state, then it is that relaxation state where your psychic channels expand. How often have you been feeling tense or edgy, but then you walk through a flower garden or a wide-open nature space and you can feel the stress just lift off your body. Many have admitted to receiving divine guidance and ideas after taking a break to head to a nature setting. Their guides were able to easily access them once the negative emotions and thoughts were reduced.

While at the gym you'll notice I was playing music while working out. Music is another element that raises your vibration, which simultaneously expands your psychic senses. People all over the globe listen to music. Music brings the people together through joy and uplifting fun. It inspires others to create, to work, and to continue on.

Exercising in nature while listening to music is a triple whammy! You're incorporating the exercise, nature, and music all at the same time. It's not rocket science to raise your vibration and increase your psychic senses. God didn't make it complicated where you have to take numerous classes, watch endless videos, and pay enormous amounts of money for a lecture or seminar on it.

Just get out there and do it.

Many will list meditation as a way to increase psychic development, but I've never technically meditated, and my psychic channels have forever been off the charts. This doesn't mean that meditation doesn't work. It just means I don't personally do it, but I do admire those that have the patience to sit Indian style in meditation for an hour and never move, since that takes enormous discipline. Some of the friends I have in the spiritual communities are also huge lovers of meditation. If you're great at meditation and that's what you prefer to do, then that will help in awakening your psychic senses. It's the relaxing element that is key here. The more relaxed you are, and the less negative feelings or thoughts plaguing you, then the easier it is to connect with spirit. It's as simple as that or perhaps not so simple if you struggle with relaxing.

If you're struggling with relaxing and removing negative feelings and thoughts, then that will need to be the first step to take care of. It's not going to happen overnight. It's a daily process of working to adjust your state of mind. This would include being able to bounce back out of a circumstance that might have upset or bothered you that day. Once you are feeling good, content, and stress free, then that's a great time to psychically connect.

While I don't sit Indian style in nature meditating for an hour, I do frequent nature settings regularly. My way of meditating is strolling through it with my hands outstretched upwards to feel God move through me, around me, and work on my well-being state, which helps me relax. Sometimes I will kick back and plop in an area on the beach and meditate on the ocean and the crashing of the waves, or I'll head to the desert and plop myself on a rock or an area with little to no people to close my eyes and allow whatever needs to come through to do so. Before I write I will close my eyes, take a deep breath in, call in my Spirit team, and center myself, but that doesn't take more than anywhere from one to five minutes max. They come in rather quickly, but this also helps in centering myself, which some meditation professionals would say is meditating.

Sometimes we get busy and distracted by the day to day practical parts of our lives, which are understandable, but then the Divine messages get lost during that time. Spirit will do their best to make the messages as known as they possibly can. Sometimes it's subtle, but other times it's so obvious that you can't miss it.

It's never been unusual for me to foresee upcoming events, but I've never looked at that as psychic fortune telling. I looked at it as an extension of me. What my Spirit team council chooses to communicate to me is often flushing in an automatic random way. I can be busy doing other things, and then a psychic alert flies in indicating something is about to take place. Other times it's something insignificant where I'm walking and clairvoyantly see a woman wearing green jogging. Ten minutes later a woman in green appears jogging down the sidewalk past me and that's the end of that. There's no reason for that foresight.

In the film *The Silence of the Lambs*, there is a scene where Clarice Starling (Jodie Foster) is communicating to Hannibal Lecter (Anthony Hopkins) through his cell. In the middle of their conversation his head lifts as if sensing something, then he looks back down glaring at her, "Dr. Chilton I presume. I believe you two know each other."

She stares at him strangely not understanding, then a beat later Dr. Chilton shows up with the authorities to escort her out of the building. In that subtle movement that audience members might've missed, it would be interpreted it that he psychically sensed Dr. Chilton was on his way. This is because there were no audible sounds of him being close and nor was he in physical view.

One of my many psychic light protection devices is to not engage with negative people or negative spirits for that matter, which should be observed whether one is a sensitive psychic being. This is something I've adopted early on in my life as a teenager, but accelerated that mantra during my twenties growing stricter about it. It also makes it challenging or frustrating for some people to get close to me right away unless they work for it. This is because I've always been doubly cautious about anyone I don't know that approaches me. I typically take a step back to observe and psychically read them to see if they are safe enough or not. I can immediately tell if someone is bathed in darkness, lower energy, or has any measure of an ulterior motive. Part of this is due to who is getting too close to my Light that it affects me physically. I need to govern my vessel with the most ultimate protection possible, because my soul comes first. The other reason is due to my distrust in others due to the childhood abuse I endured growing up and the failed relationships that followed and broke apart due to the other partner's lack of integrity. It took a great deal of soul work to evolve out of all that damage.

Combine both of those reasoning's for keeping people at arm's length and you have a supremely difficult person on your hands whose got a wall around him the size of China. This doesn't mean it's impossible since I'm surrounded by people that have been around me for decades. This means they were able to scale that wall, so it's not impossible for the strong and trustworthy. This goes both ways since those in my circles have told others that I'm one of the strongest and trustworthy people they know. You treat people how you want to be treated. It's been conveyed I'm strong and trustworthy and they mirror that right back at me, thus a beautiful long-term connection is created.

There are occasions where a negative person, spirit, or spirits can and will get into your aura and infect your light. Sometimes you can be doing everything right and it still gets on in there. It can cause all sorts of anxiety, turmoil, and a domino effect of back to back negative things happening in your life. It's just not worth the risk to invite in anyone that you suspect is infected by the Darkness, or that you psychically pick up on as having a lower energy. This is part of protecting your light, since your guides can only do so much. They'll warn you through your psychic senses and you can choose to ignore that warning or follow it. Many have admitted to ignoring it, and then later when a multitude of negative circumstances hits the fan regarding the person they will later say, "I knew something was off with that person when I met them, but I ignored it."

Mentally call in your Spirit team and ask that they surround and shield your soul from harsh energies, then pay attention to what is going on within and around you. As you tune into your psychic feeling sense you can determine through uncomfortable jolts if something or someone is on their way that you should steer clear from.

CHAPTER TWO

*Psychic Abilities are
Built into all Souls*

All babies born should immediately be handed a spirit guidebook that will help them navigate through an Earthly life effortlessly than they would without it. This includes knowing to trust and call upon God and their Spirit Guide and Guardian Angel while moving along their current life's journey. Perhaps one could assume that every parent, guardian, and teacher would pass on this knowledge, but unfortunately that is not the case with every single one of them. However, every soul that is born into a human body already has this spirit guidebook within the imprint of their soul's DNA. It's forever there waiting to be accessed by them any minute, time, or day over the course of their Earthly life.

Many people don't believe in Guides and Angels, an afterlife, God, or spirit beings. Some believe in the possibility, others believe it's forbidden to communicate with spirit guides, some are unsure if it's real, and the rest flatly believe in nothing. They believe that when you die, you die, the end.

All souls are privy to the knowledge of being surrounded by at least one guide and one angel before being born into a human body. Throughout the human developmental phase in the first number of years as a child, and through the numerous physical experiences, it is inevitable that memory loss occurs where you suppress your soul's recollections due to physical Earthly life blocks combined with what Spirit purposely blocks you from seeing until it's time. The information is present within you and never goes away. It is stored and is accessible at some point in your life. The soul memories may come through in sweeping chunks or sporadic snapshots. Psychic blocks are formed as the baby moves into childhood and beyond. By the time it reaches adulthood you may be completely psychically blocked causing complete amnesia oblivion unaware of worlds beyond Earth. There are a great many souls coming into an Earthly life again who are learning to bring that part of themselves back more than they ever had in centuries past.

There was once a time in Earth's history when we didn't have the foods, drinks, and negative emotional stresses that we have now. We weren't preoccupied by all the physical material-based distractions. We spent more time outdoors and in nature where the spirit connections were clearer then. At the same time more people are growing mindful of how certain toxic vices and toxic people negatively affect them. They are experimenting with natural herbs and remedies to find the right products that help bring a greater sense of calm focused clarity. Calm focused clarity is a state that so many are trying to achieve, but have fallen short of due to the break your back work mentality that many nations have adopted. The current work life state is to work you to death until you drop or retire, then you've got a few good years to enjoy it far beyond your prime.

This isn't about having an enormous time off to do nothing, which is one end of the extreme where you risk falling into sloth mode. The opposite extreme is working more than you have time off when it should be equally balanced. Incorporating more balance in your life in all areas where possible helps in achieving a greater sense of joy and peace, which simultaneously cracks open the psychic portal. Avoid feeling guilty about the time off you do take for yourself, because guilt is another deadly sin that creates a spirit psychic block.

Being psychic is not a special power or gift, but an extrasensory ability that every soul is born with regardless of their personal human beliefs. This ability is similar to how a human being is born breathing to stay alive. The psychic muscle part of them is a necessity and a part of the soul's make-up the way the human body has organs to physically survive. Everyone has some measure of psychic capabilities that vary from one person to the next, but no one is all knowing and powerful. The soul consciousness has the competence to receive shreds of second-sighted information, flashes of insight, and sporadic foresight, some of which needs to be deciphered and pieced together by you.

Access Spirit in Nature

Every soul on the planet has picked up on psychic hits at some point in their life, even the non-believers and those unaware they were exhibiting psychic phenomena in that instance. Going out into any nature setting with no physical distractions are where the psychic frequencies are highest. It's where God placed humankind long before structures, buildings, and technology dominated. There are endless benefits to these luxuries that humankind created, but they also play a hand at dimming and blocking spiritual communication. Getting back outdoors can assist in raising your vibration where higher psychic input resides. You are in a space that has no distractions assuming you're not going to a crowded nature locale. If you went to one of the world's most popular tourist beaches during high tourist season, then naturally you may have a tough time focusing.

Mother Nature is the perfect place for spiritual and personal enrichment of the body and soul. Spirit energy is heavy in those areas specifically because many higher spirit beings do not hang around areas bathed in negativity. They're not drawn to places like big cities, or wherever it's crowded, buildings sandwiched together, or human made creations. This is because loving spirits are drawn to light and there is little soul light that exists in physical dwellings. There are more angels and spirits watching over every flower, every grass, rock, mountain terrain than anywhere else in the world. Many nature locales contain powerful spirits hanging around those spaces.

The Native Americans were spiritual people, and America was a spiritual land at its conception. This was until it was plagued by puritanical chaotic materialistic greed filled nonsense energy that exists in the country in modern age. The spiritual part of the land sits underneath that debris. The in-tune souls can easily access it when they are centered in grace. They were and are also some of the greatest souls by having finely tuned in Mediumship abilities.

Practicing Mediumship

Partaking in Mediumship entails raising your vibration to pick up on your Guide and Angel, while your Spirit team lowers their vibration to meet you halfway. You are living in the low-density mark, and they reside in the high, so you both meet halfway, which is the medium mark.

Contrary to Biblical passages, mediumship is not of the Devil and it's not a sin, but it can invite in a negative entity. Many are conducting mediumship without trying or wanting to. They are communicating with spirit or a deceased loved one naturally because it is one of the many gifts human souls are born able to do, regardless if they believe in it or approve of it.

Practicing mediumship where you channel should be taken with the utmost seriousness due to the dangers of inviting in a negative entity. Negative spirits exist, but not in Heaven, which contains the highest love energy lights possible. They reside in one of the numerous darker layers of Hell amidst the various spiritual planes and dimensions. There are also deceased spirits stuck roaming about in the Earth plane. They strayed further from the Light avoiding it for fear of what their ego conscious mind imagines it to be. Some of them assume it's full of judgment and punishment if they had been raised in a human upbringing that cemented that false assumption into their consciousness. Some of them are unaware they passed away as they repeat the same movements like a broken record. Meanwhile, their deceased loved ones and guide and angel work to guide them into the light. Other negative spirits will hang back on the Earth plane to aggravate a human soul by attaching itself to that person. They might do this if the human being is an addict. If the negative spirit was an addict as a human being, then it will want to continue with that addiction after passing on. Therefore, it will coax the human being to use the addiction they had when living an Earthly life.

Negative spirits can and will make someone's life miserable. If you've been perpetually despondent and there are no mental health reasons for it, and it's not your general disposition, then there could be a negative spirit in the vicinity seeping itself into your aura. Sometimes just by being in the same room as you can it infiltrate your soul. When you reside in permanent fear, then you risk attracting in a negative Earth-bound spirit. Fear is what attracts a negative spirit to you as this feeds the negative spirit making it stronger in darkness.

All possibilities outside of that would need to be factored in. You cannot automatically assume it's a negative spirit, which is a deceptive trick the ego enjoys conjuring up to illicit fanfare. You would need to examine your overall state of well-being, if you've had a history of depression and anxiety, or if a life circumstance threw a curve ball at you through the death of a loved one, the loss of a job or relationship, or any other details that cannot be explained away that prompted your disposition to become indefinitely negative.

This is about those who generally have a sunny optimistic disposition, where everything is going great in their life, but one day they wake up and moodiness sets in and they cannot figure out how or why. It never seems to leave as the weeks and months pass. Nothing in that person's life can explain how this suddenly came about. Doctor checkups reveal all to be well, diet was never changed, and no life altering circumstances took place. There could be the possibility of a negative spirit that's attached itself or they are psychically picking up on something around them such as a warning.

One of the easiest ways to get rid of a negative spirit is to call in God, Jesus Christ, or the Archangel Michael to surround you with protective white light, and to extricate the spirit out of your vicinity and away from you, and take it into Heaven's holy light. If you're an experienced psychic, you may already have your own go to group for protection, but that is who I call in.

Demonic spirit entities are inhuman and the worst evil imaginable more than negative spirits. The odds of a demonic spirit being around anybody are slim having only about a 1% chance of appearing, but that's 1% out of 7 billion. The percentage of appearance is raised if you are someone that practices mediumship, channeling, or psychic readings as that can awake it from slumber. Therefore, it's crucial that you observe safe practices when it comes to psychic phenomena, including surrounding yourself with white light before you conduct a reading.

More people than ever before have been drawn into spiritual pursuits as well as the psychic phenomena field. This is fantastic pending that it's taken seriously and cautiously. The challenging side to so many doing psychic work is there are readers who have negativity surrounding their aura that is spilling out of them. There is indication they've invited a negative spirit feeder into their vicinity without realizing it. As always use caution when you conduct your readings and be sure to use safe psychic practice by shielding your space regularly and being disciplined about your environment, emotions, and surroundings.

Nailing Down Psychic Input

Some of the people that reveal the most spot-on psychic input are not necessarily professional readers, or may not even believe in it, but might be open to it. This is that friend who always seems to say things that later come true. It's a repetitive process that many around them notice. They're not doing anything in particular or trying to conduct a reading. They likely don't even know how to read using divination tools. Their soul is the tool that brings in the input naturally.

The benefit of having a strong psychic gift is to be able to make sounder choices in your life, while also warning you of danger and what and who to stay away from. Pay attention to all of your psychic senses and what comes in as you move about your day. Pray for guidance when you feel stuck on an issue and ask for signs on the best choice to make that will not leave you in a challenging state, but instead will enhance your life.

A political friend asked me, "I know you're not political, but Ossoff or Handel for Georgia?"

I said, "I have no idea what you're saying to me right now."

He clarifies, "That's whose running for the congressional seat for Georgia. I was curious what you get for them."

As someone that doesn't pay attention to the news I said, "I've never heard of them or this."

I paused in silence then said, "Handel. Whoever Handel is. That's who gets it."

Hours later he sends me a media link with the text: "Handel won. You were right. Not that it's a surprise."

How do you psychically nail the answer, how does it come to you, or what do I personally do? In this scenario, I didn't do anything. It just rushed in with the snap of a finger like it normally does. There's no special ritual. It comes in, I state it out loud, and then it's confirmed later that it came true. It's the same way I've predicted every U.S. President elect in my adult life. It's either said to me *(clairaudience)*, shown to me *(clairvoyance)*, I just know *(claircognizance)*, or pieces come in through the various psychic channels one after the other, then a year later it ends up coming to fruition.

Any soul on the planet can do that when they're paying attention to the Divine. Sometimes it just pops in out of nowhere. You don't think much of it until later when it's confirmed to be true. The reason it comes in effortlessly is because you're also not struggling to get an answer. You're just minding your own business going about your day, your vibration is high, then the psychic information slams in. Your ego isn't trying to push for an answer.

It's in hindsight where you say, "Wait a minute, okay that was a hit, but it came in so easily that I didn't recognize it as being guidance at the time."

There are many light workers and warrior of lights threaded around the world working within the political arena to help shift it away from outdated rules that no longer have any benefit in modern times. The political worlds and the people in them have enormous egos. Sometimes their hearts are in the right place, but other times they're operating from a limited space where they are too caught up in it to see clearly. That's the general perception of most of humanity, with the exception being the enlightened ones who see more than the average person. All can become enlightened if they refuse to be limited and seek to understand all aspects of human life at the time they are living it.

I had no idea what my politically based friend was talking about as I usually don't when it comes to politics. I still never knew who those two Georgia people running were. I read the headline he sent me with his text after it was confirmed to be true, but I did not read the story, as I don't care to absorb gossip or political media specifically. The other point of this is that predictions tend to be accurately foretold when you don't have any emotion invested into the question, which I don't or didn't.

You experience an accurate psychic hit easily in a situation when you don't have emotion invested into it. Your perception is crystal clear without any blocks in the way. You aren't trying to prove anything or get an answer. This is how it often sifts into your consciousness effortlessly. It's when you are completely emotionally detached from it all.

CHAPTER THREE

*Psychically Connecting
and Other Psychic Wisdom*

The higher degree of psychic connectivity, then the higher degree of sensitivities, anxiety, and insomnia one might likely have. This doesn't mean this is the case with every single person, but for the most part it tends to be the pattern. The reason is that a great deal of the ethereal spirit interruptions that take place on the soul's psychic system can cause the side effects of anxiety and insomnia. You could be battling one or both one night knowing that it has no physical explainable origin. This means things like you didn't consume caffeine late in the day that could be the reasonable reason as to why you might be experiencing anxiety or insomnia. If there is no practical cause for the anxiety or insomnia, then it could be that a psychic message is coming through your Clairsentience psychic feeling clair channel. It's your soul's job to put on the detective hat to figure out what it's connected to. It isn't something that anyone else can tell you because the message is coming through your soul and vessel. If someone called you on the phone to tell you something you wouldn't hand it to someone else to say, "What are they trying to tell me?"

When you have a higher degree and range of psychic sensitivity, then walking out into a crowd is challenging because the likelihood of absorbing or sensing erratic energy will be high. No matter how disciplined one is, and no matter how many prayers, shielding, and meditations one does, it is still near impossible to prevent these sorts of psychic stimuli from entering the soul's shield.

Due to the hyper mental and emotional activity and the psychic interference attempting to make its way into my world every second makes life more challenging. It tends to keep me on high alert all night, on and off through the night, or it will yank me awake and on guard. I've had to get up and pace or open the windows to shake it off. This lifelong insomnia was noticed early on in childhood where I'd be abruptly ripped out of sleep and lying up in bed all night acting like a funnel where the psychic vibrations from the ethers were pouring in without me able to stop it.

When planetary aspects are especially intense,

then this increases this activity. Some might not believe in the planets having this kind of effect, but the planets are like anything and everyone else where they are functioning on energy. They're not staying relatively in the same area or along similar orchestrations on its own for all eternity. There are things going on in the Universe beyond human physical comprehension that scientists are stumped on.

When someone has a higher degree of psychic sensitivity, then they can feel the rumblings within them that are connected to an erratic planetary movement in the Heavens. When this takes place, then the insomnia grows worse and I'm forced to detach and lay low as much as possible. My Spirit team eventually showed me the connection between what I was experiencing physically and the psychic activity. I had always been aware of both such as how I was feeling physically, and the psychic hits I'd receive, but it took years into my childhood and teenage years before they pointed out that they were connected to one other.

The primary way I receive spirit information is through my Clairaudience clear hearing psychic sense channel. I can think of no further proof of an afterlife or psychic related incidents when I'm hearing my Spirit council talk to me as clearly as anyone else does. They've said things to me that I've replied out loud with to someone only to discover what I said was true or eventually comes true. When this is the regular way you communicate with spirit since childhood, then you are instantaneously used to it. I had never done any special invocation or other psychic taught practice. It was just happening regardless of what I was doing.

You can note by the previous illustrations as to how much work is involved being a fine tuned in psychic sponge. It isn't necessarily a fun thing to absorb so much more than the average person.

As you become more accustomed to the knowledge that your soul is separate from your body, but that it's also connected, then it gets easier to put on the psychic detective hat naturally in order to decipher if what you're experiencing is psychic activity coming through or your ego or something else.

When a medium is called to investigate a haunting in a house, they will not immediately believe the house is haunted. They will first investigate the house to see if it could be something else like a bad pipe or any other physical explain away before then moving that into the next level which is metaphysical and psychic phenomena. This is how you would act while putting on the psychic detective hat.

The following list is an example of some of the things that can explain away the reasons for repetitive anxiety, insomnia, and other negative emotions before you can conclude that it may be psychic activity attempting to come through:

• You received some bad news that day or recently pertaining to your life or someone close to you. This could include things like the loss of a job, relationship breakup, passing of a loved one, legal issues, you have to give a speech/perform, any kind of personal or professional life issue can cause it, etc.

• Examine the foods you've been eating since that will influence your system.

• Did you drink alcohol, smoke/ingest weed, or take any kind of drug that alters your perception.

• Look at the pills or supplements you take each day or might have taken the day you experienced the unexplainable activity.

• Talk to a Doctor to rule out any kind of medical condition or other health issue going on.

When you've ruled out every possible physical reason, then it could be there is psychic activity and paranormal interference coming in. The activity seems to increase at night because you're not distracted by the day to day practical world. You're alone, quiet, and motionless with your thoughts.

When the psychic activity or challenging planetary aspects rear its ugly head, then everything in my life comes to a complete stand still during that time, no writing done, nothing. Most meetings and appointments get cancelled. My strict exercise regimen gets hit, which is unusual since I'll exercise and work out even if I'm dead. If I'm too out of it due to the lack of sleep, then I'm basically useless. I can write easy personal emails and make friend phone calls since they don't care what state I'm in and understand my nature. Other than that, I use that time to lay low and hang out in nature. I will sometimes lie down in a nature setting and allow the nature spirits energy to envelop and heal me.

During those heavy anxiety moments, I also end up on high alert. The fun part or not so fun part is the insomnia gets out of control. Eyes wide open vigilant like an animal. That part is tough because too much psychic overload is flying in at once. When certain testy planetary energy is in motion, I can feel that friction without knowing there is a tough transit going on. Every single time this happens I'm never surprised to find it's an unstable planetary time. There isn't anything I can do to make it stop, as the energy pull is too strong. I just have to ride it out and wait for the storm to pass, and it will lighten up because as it is said...this too shall pass. Being a fine tuned in psychic sponge means you will take the good with the bad. The challenges for me are that it is constantly fluctuating and moving every second that I can feel it.

No spirit writing or work involving my mental aptitude takes place during those aggravated times. That is temporarily closed for refurbishment throughout the days of little sleep. It's different than the regular bouts of spiritual maintenance I do every so often the way you take your car in for maintenance.

When anything is especially intense it's best to be patient and ride it out as much as possible. There have been the rare times when my insomnia goes on for several consecutive nights. I'm laying up all night going mentally crazy and frustrated. I need my disciplined nightly eight hours of sleep to function at optimum levels. I know that I cannot continue one more night like that.

As the sun sets on day four of bad sleep and the darkness comes upon me, I mumble with the horrid anxiety to God and my Spirit team, "Please let me sleep tonight, please, please, please. You have to help. I cannot do this one more night. I can't. Bring everybody in if you have to."

And thank God I finally sleep that night. The despair is vastly great at that point that Divine intervention finally comes through. The sound sleep feels so good that I'm stunned because it feels like being saved.

Once I sleep fully through the night again, then I'm back to peak levels physically, mentally, emotionally, and spiritually. The spirit communication starts flooding in effortlessly and clearly upon waking, then I spend that day catching up on days lost.

It can be strange during that period when spirit communication is quieter, but as soon as I fully sleep it is like the door slams open and the Light floods in again. The second my eyes open after the first night's sleep, then the channel is fully open and in movement. I smile and say, "Thank you, God! I'm back. Rejoice!"

Some measure of good sound sleep is essential to psychically and divinely connect on a deeper level since the physical health is connected to psychic health.

Developing a Relationship with Spirit

I typically feel the strongest jolt when the Holy Ghost moves through me. Those moments are memorable because it's that connection which produces uplifting love, joy, and serenity. I'm not someone known for shedding tears that easily, so when I do in this case it's to illustrate how powerful it is that it shakes me to my soul's core. Swiftly detach from your ego in order to move into the face of Spirit and back out again as needed. It is also how one learns to tame the beast of the darkness of ego

Calling in my Spirit team, I don't typically conduct any special ceremonies, even though I have friends in the spiritual community that do. Everyone has their own ways of doing things they prefer. My method has always been on the simpler side where I just plain ask a guide or angel to come in for me the way I would ask anyone for something.

For example, there was a period in my life where my union with Archangel Michael was growing stronger over time. It wasn't like day one the request for him to be my personal body-soul guard happened and it was done. He was coming in sporadically at first. As time went on my relationship bond with him grew stronger that it became permanent on its own.

At one point we had the conversation where we made this united pact that he would be there permanently. Part of that was also because I get distracted with Earthly life situations and things would happen. If he was already next to me full time, then it was just easier for all of us to have him be part of the team. He wanted to the way God wants a relationship with His children.

There was a point when I made a firm request with Archangel Michael. I invited him in permanently through an invitation that was real the way you would commit to a love partner. You want this, they want this, and it is done. It's also similar to what Christ followers mean when they say, "Have you asked Jesus to come into your heart?"

Some people don't know what that means, but it's like my relationship with Archangel Michael. He becomes a part of you as Jesus Christ is a part of me as well too. I love Christ's goodness, compassion, and forgiveness. He also helps me stay centered amidst an inner and outer world of chaos.

With Archangel Michael, this is the same way you meet someone new who is going to end up being one of your close friends. It's not like you're instantly best friends on the first day - at least not in my life. It's over time as you're both showing up for the relationship does it start to grow stronger. This was the same way it was with Archangel Michael. It was allowing him in on occasion. I was thinking, "Okay let me see what you can do and why do you want to be here?"

I'd try him on like a pair of jeans that I'd wear occasionally, until I started to wear them every day by spending more time with him, then the relationship bond started to grow. This concept is similar with all I've connected with whether in spirit or in people. It's the same way someone develops any relationship that grows stronger over time. It's spending more time with them and developing a legitimate loyal relationship with them. Today he's part of the air that I breathe. I can't imagine him not being around anymore. I'm too used to his presence and him being around for so long. I would know if he ever left, but he hasn't. I don't think twice about it. I wake up and he's already there even if I'm not coherent yet.

Connecting with Spirit

Some psychics or mediums meditate to get into a trance like state to connect with Spirit. The reason this is an effective method for them is because you're taking at least a few minutes to quiet your mind. You're silencing everything around you in order to have a stronger connection with the Other Side. When you quiet your thoughts and the noise of the outside world, then there is room for Spirit and God to come rushing in. Silencing everything includes removing any traces of negativity from your aura, thoughts, and feelings. If you're upset about something, then this will make it difficult to channel or psychically connect until you let that go and release it. It's best to wait until you're in a relaxed state, even if that means pushing the psychic or medium session to another day.

When you've moved into a state of Divine reception, then the messages and guidance from above flows into your soul through one of your psychic clair sense channels and the connection is made. The first step to getting closer to channeling naturally is by being aware of your own soul and what's outside of it. When you pay attention and notice all the physical distracting noises, then you're able to diminish those sounds. You can do that when you're out and about in a busy area such as a street or at a mall.

Some of the ways of fine tuning your clear hearing Clairaudience psychic sense channel would include listening to sounds that are typically grating on a sensitive person. For the purpose of understanding the distinctive differences between the psychic channel and physical channel it's helpful to do it for a few minutes.

Perk up your ears hearing the noisy symphonic physical sounds coming from the rumbling of cars, tires skidding, garbage cans banging, sirens going off, people talking or shouting, and so on. Notice the distracting energy on your phone and the things you aim your focus towards while on it. The key is being *aware* when it has become a distraction. Once you're able to notice these differences, you not only realize how distracted the planet is, but you're then able to work on dissolving those sounds from your mind to tune it out. When it is tuned out, then the noise level of spirit begins to rise.

Spirit is already loud because they're in the same room with you, but when it sounds as if they're non-existent, far away, or muted, it is because you're either psychically blocked, or the sounds of the physical part of the world are turned up way too high around you. Those sounds include the noise of your own thoughts. It's like you're blasting your music at home while you and a guest are trying to talk over it. You keep saying, "What?" You then turn the music down a little in order to hear one another. Turning the physical distractions down enables one to hear the voice of Heaven clearer.

I've been driving with my music blaring while simultaneously communicating with Spirit effortlessly because their words travel over the chords of music for me. The downfall is I'm blasting the music. There have been times that I'm asking them what they said through telepathy. I'd repeatedly say, "Say that again."

One would finally shout, "Turn it down!"

I'm thrown off reaching to turn my own stereo down, then I can hear them clearly.

CHAPTER FOUR

Communicating with the Divine

No spirit being in Heaven can interfere with someone's free will choice unless they are specifically requested to by that soul, or if the decision the soul is making will result in their premature death. Heaven sits back and watches human souls paint themselves into a corner hoping a rush of clarity seeps in. This is why you must formerly request Spirit intervention, guidance, and assistance. When you invite any spirit in Heaven to step in, then your life becomes a bit easier than if you didn't ask for Divine assistance. Challenges are inevitable on Earth, but moving through those challenges more swiftly helps when you have your Spirit team on your side.

Pushing for an answer from the Divine will

block the ability to pick up on incoming messages and guidance. Anything connected to fear will sever the connection line. Psychic communication hits filter in when you're in a calm non-judgmental uplifting state. You let go of any resistance while avoiding the desire to push for an answer. Work on regular vibration raising exercises that include clearing your mind, body, and soul of any toxic debris. This can be done in meditation or stillness, as well as through the elimination of vices that you know are holding you back from achieving.

Sit or stand in silence releasing intrusive toxic thoughts and feelings until you are a clear vessel to absorb Divine input. Seeing or hearing celestial wisdom clearly is restricted if you're constantly listening to or paying attention to the noise around you. The noise is everybody else, the media, your negative thoughts and feelings, and the physical concrete world sounds. Physical world sounds are things like car noises, airplanes, and crowd chatter. This doesn't include the sounds of the ocean waves crashing and hitting the sand, or the wind blowing against the side of a mountain. Turn the obtrusive physical sounds all off if you want to truly hear God.

Find a quiet place to sit and be still in prayer or meditation. Allow your Spirit team to know what's bothering you and what it is that you would like help with. You can also ask if there is anything you need to know that day. If you can get out into a nature locale, then this is ideal whether it's your backyard or a park. This would be somewhere you can be alone in God's paradise to release. Take continuous slow deep breaths in and release it all, because you don't need to carry that harsh energy around. This is done until you feel more relaxed and centered.

When you feel defensive, emotionally hurt, full of anger, depressed, then Spirit always advises you to get out in nature. The word nature needs to be emphasized because going outdoors to a crowded mall is not what is going to center you. Find balance in those instances and detoxify your soul and body.

If you're doing this at home, then open the space around you to bring in your Spirit team. You can do this through meditation or quiet time. Play uplifting powerful spiritual background music, light candles, incense, or whatever you choose to bring you and your soul into a centered space. Be patient, give it time, and call them in.

If you pull cards to help with the connection, then you can't pull cards quickly and assume the guides are there. Call them in and give them time to come in, then pull the cards. Don't control what you hope the answer will be, but allow it to flow in when you're in an emotionally detached space. Release any unforgiveness in your heart about yourself or others. Let it go by visualizing it moving out of you and upward towards Heaven for transmutation, so that the weight of that toxin is released.

Paying attention to the messages and guidance coming in from your Spirit team can help you navigate through your Earthly life much more swiftly. They can help you recognize when something in your life is intended to end, or when you're to act on a circumstance, and so on. They can assist when you learn to pay attention and recognize those hits they're giving you. No one can do that for you.

You may go to a psychic reader for answers, but may not always get the messages you seek. This is because in the end it is up to you to decide how your life is going to go and what decision you are to make. You're not a puppet on strings that can be controlled by another being. An impeccable psychic reader, healer, and counselor can give you clarity and direction, but it is up to you to make the ultimate decision as to the best option. It is up to you to make that decision for your life. It is your life and you are the manager and CEO of it. This is the same way an extraordinary CEO at a company will hear other input or ideas from the employees, but ultimately it will be the CEO's decision as to the best course of action. This is the same way you manage your life. You may bounce ideas off as to what you should do about something with other people. You'll take that into account, and mull it around in your mind, ask your Spirit team for guidance on what to do, then eventually make the decision based on where you're getting the strongest vibrational pull.

You can minimize the difficulties in your life when you ask for heavenly help and guidance, and then tune in to that still place within where these answers reside. You don't need someone else to give you confirmation because you have the confirmation. God didn't make it difficult where you have to go to people for the answers. You were instilled with built in psychic sense clair channels so that you can be in constant communication with your Spirit team any time, day, or night.

Take a deep breath in, focus on centering yourself, elevate your faith believe, and mentally strip away any fear-based thoughts that get in the way of preventing blessings from falling into your vicinity. You are not alone or being ignored even when if it sometimes feels that way. Allow any negative toxicity around you to dissolve away. This will crank up the volume of the angels and then God comes flowing in effortlessly.

If the answer is not present at that moment, then give it time. Pay attention as you move forward in life for the answer. Sometimes the answer doesn't come in right away when you ask for it. It can come in at a later date. It can be days, weeks, months, and even years later. Although, the latter is rare, the years later is typically when the event you're asking about isn't going to take place until further into the future. Because it's so far out, you're unable to psychically pick up on it. It's only as you grow closer to the date does the information begin to become clearer and stronger without breaking away from that energy vibration.

Be granted the wisdom to understand why events beyond your control take place. Let God and the angels be your driver when it feels as if you have no more strength to persevere. They will re-charge and re-ignite your soul when you request it. Talk to God and your Spirit team daily and pour your heart out. You are heard whether you believe you are or not. You can communicate your request with your thoughts, in prayer, out loud, and in writing. It doesn't matter how you communicate, but that you do.

What's been on your mind lately causing you inner turmoil? This is a clue as to what you need to let go of. Have the intention of letting go of it and releasing it to Heaven for positive transformation. Unhappiness in any area of your life is also a way to discover what it is you need to change. Have you forever been unhappy with your job? What action steps are you comfortable with making to change this? Pour your heart out to God and your Spirit team as to what's bothering you and ask for guidance on steps they want you to take. Often when you ask for guidance you may be requested to act with something that will help bring it closer.

Write to Your Spirit Team

One highly effective way of communicating with your Spirit team is through writing. When you communicate with any higher being in Heaven, you are communicating with God by default since they are extensions of Him.

When you sit down to write out what you'd like to say to those on the Other Side, there is a stronger intention and force behind it. This force intention is energy that carries solid weight. You find your intention to be stronger with your thoughts, while someone else prefers to say it out loud.

I communicate using the various ways one can communicate, but I've found it efficient when I write it out. Part of this is because I'm a writer and it's easier for me to communicate through the written word. I'll sit down and open a new email message box and address it as you would with anyone.

"Dear...."

I'm notorious for emailing myself hundreds of letters to God, my Spirit team, and myself.

You can write a letter to a departed loved one who you miss dearly, because they can read what you are writing when you grant them permission. The addressing of the letter is granting them permission to read it. When you request heavenly support or guidance, you are heard the instant you call out to them. It doesn't matter if the request is big or small because you are heard regardless. You cannot get away with a lie in Heaven the way you can with others on the planet. You might write or say one thing, but what's in your heart is what's heard and understood to be the truth by any spirit being.

Sometimes when you're in a discombobulated state, it's easier to sit down and write it out in an email, on a notepad, or wherever you usually write. I email my letters to God and my Spirit team to myself and file it away in a folder marked, "Angels". This is where thousands of letters and private communications with my team live. I do the same with jotting down psychic information I'm getting and emailing it to myself. When I've reverted to those emails, I've found everything that I jotted down ended up coming to fruition, but I had forgot about it when I originally jotted it down.

Writing instead of speaking or thinking the words can help you articulate it more efficiently. It forces you to stop for a moment and type out what you're experiencing. This is also therapeutic giving you a sense of calm. Any sudden feeling of serenity is the angels easing the stress you're feeling as you write it out. You've also moved into a state of stillness, which helps them to get to work on you easier when you're less erratic or restless. It can also help you make sense of the words you're putting out into the Universe.

As a writer I find writing assists with bringing on clarity and focus, but not everyone is comfortable with writing something out. I have friends who are naturally sociable verbally, or do radio shows and podcasts, so they prefer to speak the words rather than write them out. These are the gifted speakers that dominate through voice rather than the pen.

One friend like that has said in the past repeatedly, "I talk. You write."

Those friends tend to leave me long voice messages that cut them off since there is no more space. They have to call back and continue in another voice box. There are times I call them to say, "I want to talk about this, but I'm going to write you first, then we'll discuss it."

Everyone has different ways of communicating from one another that dominate. This is the same way all souls have varying psychic gifts from one another that also govern. In the end it doesn't matter how you communicate with Heaven, but that you do.

Tuning into Divine Messages

The clearest way of knowing if it's a Divine message or not is if it ends up coming true. The other ways are it's felt with a layer of uplifting love around it even when it's a warning. This may seem like common sense, but you would be surprised that the obvious answer is not what is generally thought of or known to be the one. Some believe that psychic input must be complicated and difficult to distinguish, but the truth is ones Guides and Angels do their best to try and convey it to you as simply as possible. When that tap on the head to pay attention to something doesn't work, then they try other ways such as throwing up repeated symbols and signs to get you to notice it. If God has been knocking on your door for some time, then take the hint and open it and let Him in.

A Divine message continuously comes in until you pick up on the repetitive theme happening. This prompts you to take notice and focus on it. It will continue to come in periodically as it pushes you to action. Take steps towards making something happen if that's the gut hunch you continue to receive. The voice of the ego will cause some form of sabotage even if it's miniscule, whereas Heavenly messages will never cause drama or harm to you or anyone else around you. A Divine message brings good, positive, high vibrational feelings to you or another person even if it's a warning.

When it feels like your connection with Spirit is non-existent where you're not picking up on anything, then that's typically a sign that you're too weighed down or distracted by physical and external matters or desires. If you're experiencing any form of negativity whether in emotions or thought processes, then that's a block. Being mired in any of kind of physical distraction will temporarily dim or cut off the communication line with the Other Side. It makes it seem as if you're not picking up on anything or you're being ignored, which is never true because Spirit is always communicating with you regardless if you can hear them or not.

The Spirit communication gradually opens up when you start releasing and letting go of unnecessary toxic distractions, as well as negative feelings and thoughts. If you're not hearing messages or guidance, then examine your life and make note of what's bothering you or distracting you in the physical world. Work on acknowledging it, then releasing it and letting it go. The answer as to what is creating the block is usually right in front of you. If you have more than one issue bothering you, then you have to let it all go one by one in order to allow the communication to come rushing in. Lifestyle shifts and changes will need to be made in areas where you are able to make them. Some changes you'll be able to make right away, while others will be more challenging, or it will take longer depending on what it is.

Seeking Psychic Input from Others

When one thinks of psychics, they immediately connect that to someone being able to predict your future. Your future is set based on your soul contract coupled with your free will choices. You are creating and designing your own future. Do you need someone to tell you when you'll meet your next soul partner? Or when you'll move into a new home or get that new job? Avoid getting stuck in the cycle of waiting around for something to transpire. Be proactive in making what you want to happen.

You might go to an intuitive friend or a psychic to help give you the messages and guidance you seek that you're unclear on, but it's up to you to come to the answer on your own time. Jumping ahead to get the answer instead of doing the work by moving through the troubling experience can be met with disappointment or confusion.

I've heard or read from others that a psychic reading they had was inaccurate or didn't give them the information they sought out. While others may say that it helped give them peace of mind, but only time will tell if it ends up coming to fruition. If the reading helped give you a lift, then its job and intention were beneficial. Sometimes talking it out with someone or receiving an objective point of view from someone who cares can help immensely.

When your life is not where you want it to be, then you seek out a psychic reader hoping to give you some good news. It's rare that one will go to a reader when they're on cloud nine on all physical aspects of their life from career, love, finances, health, and home. If you go to a poor psychic, then you can get sucked into the reader giving you false hope. You want to avoid the scam readers. Those might be the ones that overcharge you for their services, or tell you there is a curse around you that only they can remove if you pay them more money. Avoid readers that consistently try to get you to purchase more stuff from them. Those who are where they want to be will go to a reader if they love the craft or desire some fun uplifting soul affirming guidance, since everyone is a work in progress. There are endless stories of people who have a great career, tons of money, and a beautiful love relationship, yet they still feel unhappy inside or spiritually bankrupt. This only further cements that true authentic happiness starts from within the core of your soul, then you expand that allowing it to work its way outwardly.

Noticing Divinely Guided Synchronicities

Notice the little synchronicities placed in front of you by Spirit that lead to what you're intended to act on next. Bumping into the same person repeatedly isn't always an accident. This doesn't necessarily mean colleagues where it's expected that you would naturally be bumping into them daily, but it does mean that person you continuously bump into in passing on a beach, while shopping, at a park, on the sidewalk, at a coffee and tea shop, at the gym, and so on. Consider if that person continues to notice you with a mutual glimmer in their eye as if to positively acknowledge you in a way they don't seem to be doing with anyone else around. Maybe it's a new friendship, a love relationship, or acquaintance soul mate intended to relay a message to you that positively enlightens or shifts the direction on your path. Perhaps it's a new business networking connection, or maybe it's the next long-term love relationship. Be open to the signs and symbols floating around your auric world that comes through as messages from other people. Sometimes these other people are not initially aware they are messengers. They too are picking up on the guidance and messages from their own Spirit team.

While driving one morning, I was listening to a popular open-minded preacher in an earpiece. At the same time on my car stereo I had rock music playing low, which I could hear in my left ear that was open to hear external sounds. The preacher pulled out a verse and said the number "seventeen". At the same time the rock singer on the stereo sang the word, "seventeen". The synchronous way that the number seventeen was said at the same time alerted me to pay attention to it. This is one example in how these signs and symbols sift in front of you to take notice.

When I mentioned this was an open-minded preacher, it wasn't to be confused with those hate filled vengeance preacher's that cast judgment on people, which I would never absorb or listen to.

This preacher focuses on love never having uttered a hate filled word before. The good ones are out there when you search for them.

Endings and New Beginnings

Your Spirit team guides you down the best path for your highest self. They'll send signals of warning when you're in danger or if you're insisting on going down a road that's less desirable. If something doesn't work out, then look at that as a blessing where it didn't happen for a reason. There could've been hidden dangers that you were not noticing or paying attention to.

Let's say you or someone you know is going to meet a potential date with someone new you haven't met before. You find you have to push yourself to meet up with this person, or you feel unexcited with challenging feelings around that, then this is a clue not to go. I know that might sound like common sense, but when you're in the throes of a decision like that you'd be surprised to find the ego isn't paying attention to the best course of action. You're wrestling with indecisiveness about it. Unless you're filled with excitement, then don't waste your time or the other persons. Some have found they would ignore that guidance, go on the meeting only to realize immediately that it's going to be disastrous or a waste of time. As you're driving back home, you're thinking, "Why did I go? I knew it was a mistake beforehand. If I race home, I'll be able to catch the late-night show."

If an ex-lover is moving out of the country, the state, or far away from you, then look at that in a positive way. If you're single, the angels could be moving this person away from you so that you are open to a new person they are bringing in that is more aligned with who you are today. You may think you've been ready and had moved on from a relationship, but Spirit can see the residual ex energy still lingering in your aura. They have to get rid of this ex physically, so that this new person they want to bring you can come in.

This same concept applies to anyone intended to come in, including friendships, acquaintances, or new business connections. At the time it's happening you might be filled with sadness or grief not wanting this ex to leave, but as time goes on and new brighter circumstances come into your life, you realize why this person had to be sent away. You had outgrown them, but didn't know it because they were still hanging around. It was only after they left that you discover your time with them had long ended. That person's essence in your life was holding you back from these other brighter experiences screaming to get in, even if you disagree with that notion at the time.

Only in hindsight after time has passed do you start to realize the changes that took place after the previous circumstance was completely dissolved. Sometimes this ex is drawn away because they have personal soul lessons they need to learn. Other times it's Heaven's way of helping you become less dependent on someone else and to start relying on you. You can't do that when this other person is still hanging around.

Life is full of beginnings and endings, doors closing and windows opening. This kind of drastic change can bring on all sorts of emotions from excitement to fear depending on whether or not the change is purposely done at your own hands or if it was the Universe that was shutting the door on things you weren't ready to part with. When that happens, it is done so for a reason, even if that reason is not yet evident. One of the many ways to change and grow is to transform completely. This gets you out of any stuck energy like a rut or stagnancy. This way you can move onto brighter pastures and circumstances that want to come into your life.

CHAPTER FIVE

The Psychic Clair Senses

When any spirit being in Heaven communicates with you, the tone is direct, full of love, and uplifting, even if they are warning you of danger. They communicate firmly, while your ego communicates with uncertainty, anger, or any other disapproving negative emotion. Your Spirit team will never advise you to do something that ends up hurting you or someone else.

Your Spirit Guide, Guardian Angel, God, or any entity or spirit communicates with you through your senses. Your senses are not to be confused with your physical senses, but these senses are interwoven between your physical body and your soul. These senses are also referred to as *clairs*, which means 'clear'. It is being a clear psychic channel with the planes and dimensions beyond the Earth plane. There are over a dozen clair points in your soul, but there are four primary clairs. Many have one or two dominate clairs, but those who work on opening the other clairs have all four clair channels opened up and even some of the others. It takes work and a lifestyle change to keep them open since a clair can easily dim or close depending on your life circumstance. Since you are an energy vessel, when they turn to anger or sadness, then this is simultaneously closing the psychic clairs. If you are suddenly lifted in grand feelings of joy, love, and peace, then your psychic clair senses begin to expand. How you think, feel, and navigate Earthly life influences both your spiritual and physical body.

Your clairs are also considered to be an extra sensory perception, because the clair senses reach places beyond what your physical senses can do. You hear the voices of spirit, but your physical ears are not hearing them. It is your spirit soul senses that hear them. The extra sensory part of the equation is the extra psychic sense that is beyond the physical.

You receive a telepathic hit when you are thinking of someone you haven't communicated with for some time, then suddenly they contact you out of the blue to say they were thinking of you and wanted to reach out. You might say to them, "How weird as I was just thinking about you!"

Your Spirit team is implanting this psychic information in your mind for a reason. Maybe it's to remind you of the good that existed in that person and how they made you feel. Perhaps it's to bring you both together again to resolve old issues and bring the connection to proper closure. Or it could be that you or this other person has information or wisdom that is passed onto you when you have that conversation. Sometimes it can simply be a good, positive, fun discussion that uplifts you out of a mood you've been in or it's you that uplifts them. When a great deal amount of time passes with no contact from someone, then often that gives both parties clarity they were unable to see while in the connection.

You both have a telepathic communication line flowing back and forth between your souls. Telepathy is Claircognizant communication that is verbally unspoken. Claircognizance is a clear knowing about something you're not versed in. It is also the area that thoughts are transmitted psychically that later comes true. Telepathy might be where someone is deeply thinking of you and is unknowingly transmitting the informational thoughts to you. This wakes you up to suddenly be thinking of them. You hadn't for quite some time, then out of nowhere they flash into your mind. You later discover when you reach out to them that they had been thinking of you the week prior.

Some have admitted they've noticed that when you're thinking of someone that they are likely thinking of you. While this can certainly be true, typically one of you ends up reaching out to the other at some point not long afterwards. The telepathy has a measure of psychic foresight to it. You can also have telepathic communication with a soul on the Other Side such as a departed loved one. The departed loved one is sending you a psychic signal that they are around you and guiding you on something. You then suddenly get a strong flush of their presence in your mind that you hadn't for a while. This could be where you are also missing them deeply out of nowhere. This deeply missing them component is a signal that they're with you at that moment. You're feeling their presence so deeply that it might sadden you because you're missing them, but that should be a joyful feeling to know they are doing amazing and have stopped in to say hello. They didn't intend to sadden you or upset you.

It is assumed that someone with psychic abilities has a rare gift, but these gifts have been given to every living soul including the most rigid Atheist or most heinous human being on the planet plagued with Darkness. They have psychic abilities deep down in their soul. No one is more special than anyone else where psychic abilities are concerned. Everyone is psychic and has the ability to connect. Some connect easier than others or in different ways than someone else does. Someone might have a stronger Clairvoyance channel than someone that has strong Clairaudience. Everyone has these psychic clair gifts, but each person's gifts might vary. It's up to the individual to discover which of their psychic clair senses are the strongest. Some people might not have to work as hard to re-open their clair senses or they live a life that has minimal blocks in their environment.

All souls have psychic gifts, but you're not

paying attention to this Divine input of information if you are buried deeply in the physical world. Living on this testy battlefield of a planet comes with an array of blocks that reduces your psychic gifts. The good news is that one's psychic gifts never go away. They might dim or darken, but they're accessible to anyone who chooses to re-awaken that part of their soul.

The Four Psychic Clair Senses

The Four Main psychic clair senses are *Clairvoyance, Clairaudience, Clairsentience,* and *Claircognizance.* Read the basic descriptions in the coming pages in this chapter in order to pinpoint what best describes you. The descriptions are the basic generalizations of how to recognize you or someone else as having that clair.

The psychic clair senses are present deep in the DNA of your soul since it is a part of you, but it just needs to be worked out if it's unnoticed. It's the same way someone who goes to the gym regularly to stay healthy, fit, and build muscle. If they suddenly stopped going or working out and exercising, then the muscle would lessen over time and one's health would gradually deteriorate. Psychic clair senses work in that same respect. You treat it like a muscle that needs to be built, strengthened, and taken care of regularly. Your physical body can build muscle or tone when you exercise. Your clair channels work in the same way. When you regularly exercise a psychic clair, then you build its muscle over time. You do the work out maintenance as you would if you were exercising regularly to strengthen your physical body and overall health.

Clairvoyance

Clairvoyance means "Clear Seeing" (or "Clear Vision"). You have clairvoyance if you receive visual images, cues, or impressions sifting through your mind's eye. Your mind's eye is also called the third eye. The third eye looks like an eye and is located between your two physical eyes, but slightly raised above it. It cannot be seen with your physical eyes. If you close your eyes and focus on seeing your third eye, then you should be able to see it with practice. It is behind the area between where your eyes are located turned right side up. When you see violet light around the third eye area or in your peripheral vision, then this is a positive indicator that your clairvoyance is opening up.

The psychic images are projected through clairvoyance like a mini movie playing for you. Someone might be born into this lifetime blind through their physical eyes, yet they receive powerful psychic visual impressions through their third eye. The third eye is where your clairvoyance channel shows you the psychic messages and guidance your Spirit team is communicating to you. You would know whether or not the visual images were your imagination or a psychic hit if what you're seeing ends up coming true.

Clairvoyant messages often need to be decoded. The reason is the communication is being brought to you through a moving visual picture or still image. The significance of the illustration does not always mean what is being shown to you. It is up to you to decipher what the message is supposed to be about. You might be shown a ship leaving a harbor, which might make one assume they are going on a cruise. The obvious answer is not always the right one when it comes to clairvoyance. The ship could be a metaphor to how you're feeling rather than a literal message. Having psychic senses, especially clairvoyance, requires one to be able to delve deep. It isn't enough to open up the psychic clairs, but there's a great deal of regular work going on that you're expected to do.

If you are someone that has vivid dreams that you recall long after you've woken up from sleep, then this is a sign that you may have strong clairvoyant abilities without realizing it.

Here's one minor example of clairvoyance. You are asleep and having a dream where you are walking the streets at night. There are hundreds of snakes and cobras moving about around you attacking everyone except you. As a clairvoyant it's your goal to decipher what this moving image means, because it's highly unlikely that this is an image showing you of what's to come. It can mean that you're a rising successful star in your profession who is untouchable, but this is not met without enemies. There is someone or many who are or will be jealous of you. This could be one way to interpret the dream of the snakes attacking everyone around except you. You might have to do some research to find out the significance symbolism of snakes as well as snakes that attack, and all of the details in the dream, such as it being nighttime. It's a good idea to keep a journal or notepad near you to jot down your dreams or any random psychic hits you receive throughout the day. As mentioned earlier, I email it to myself so that it's recorded down for later viewing. You will forget the psychic hits unless it's written down.

I saw the love interest that was coming to me in grave detail. I jotted down the person's name, stats, job, the time frame they were showing up, and even the birthdate! I filed it away emailing it to myself and went on with life. A year later I developed a crush on someone that I felt a strong pull towards immediately and I know they felt it too, because I could psychically feel that. Months later as I got to know this person, I was suddenly prompted to go back to one of my readings a year earlier. I was stunned to find out this person was the love interest! Everything matched up from name, birthdate, job, stats, height, build, eyes, hair, and on and on. I had forgot about the reading because I'm doing dozens of reads a week that are getting filed away. Moral of the story is to write down what you get as soon as possible. A well-known medium friend of mine has said to me in private, "You read better for yourself than I've seen anyone do."

But I'm also a believer that if I can, then anyone can if they tune in and focus.

You have clairvoyance if you also see spirits from the Other Side. It looks as if they're in front of you or to the side of you in your peripheral vision. They don't look like physical human beings, which is the way they're portrayed in some Hollywood films. They look more opaque or translucent. You may even see them as lights or sparkling lights in your peripheral vision. When I clairvoyantly see a spirit initially, they will look like a human being for the first few seconds until I do a double take, then I realize they are translucent. They're not translucent on the Other Side, but the way it comes through the spirit planes in front of you it appears as if they are.

For some your conscious will block your abilities to see spirits for fear of seeing a deceased spirit looking the way they had when they passed away. They might have died a violent death such as a murder or car accident. The spirit is fine and doesn't look like that on the Other Side, but they can appear how they choose to for anybody. This sometimes includes how they looked when they died or the age they passed away. If they died a violent death, then they might appear that way to be recognizable to you.

Someone's grandfather passed away at ninety-two years old, but when he crossed over, he appears in top form looking like a young twenty-five to thirty-four-year-old human being. He might appear ninety-two years old in human years to a psychic medium in order to relay what is coming through on a reading for someone. You might not know who the medium was talking about if your grandfather appeared the way he did at twenty-five years old. He would look significantly different if he appeared as he does on the Other Side.

Generally, the deceased loved one is brought to top form back home and appears stronger and more vibrant than ever before. In human age it tends to be late twenties to early thirties. Any human physical, mental, or emotional issue is dissolved when you cross over. For example, if someone had to wear glasses their entire Earthly life. Those glasses are no longer needed when they cross over. If someone suffered from depression or mental health issues, then when they cross over, they are brought back to their natural soul state of all love, joy and peace in a big vibrant way.

Clairvoyant messages can also come through your psychic channel as symbols, numbers, colors, letters, words, and pictures that have a meaning to you or someone else. It can be something from the past, the present, or future. Those who have clairvoyance tend to daydream as well. These daydreams may be random, or they may be images of what's happened, what's happening, or what's to come. They see their own future as if it's a vision board of what is to take place at some point. When someone tells a clairvoyant friend a story, the clairvoyant is living the story as if it's happening to them personally. They see the story as if they are the main character. The clairvoyance channel is incredibly alive that it can be challenging in this way to mentally see what someone is describing to you.

Clairsentience

Clairsentience means "clear feeling" (or "clear sensing"). This is when you feel the psychic messages, guidance and impressions coming through you from Spirit and Heaven. Those that have high clairsentience might walk into a building and feel as if all eyes are on them even though no one is looking. Or they might pick up on an uneasy sense of foreboding that tells them to get out of a particular place or away from someone. They perceive danger is about to happen and then it soon does. They also intuit good stuff that is coming into their vicinity as well, which ends up happening. You might have a strong upbeat joyful feeling that the job you want is going to come about and then this later comes true.

Having clairsentience is when your Spirit team communicates messages and guidance through your feelings, emotions, and senses. It's not something that is heard or seen, but felt within you. Those that consider themselves to be highly intuitive, empathic, or super sensitive are more likely to have a strong Clairsentience psychic channel.

You might be the kind of person that becomes emotionally upset when someone you're interested in romantically is not reciprocating that interest. You text and email this person regularly hoping to illicit a response that is satisfying to you. Yet the object of your desire is casual in their reply when communicating with you, or they continuously drop the ball with your text dalliance. You question whether or not they're truly interested in you.

When they throw you a bone and click 'like' on one of your social media posts, then you're suddenly on cloud nine believing they're interested in you. Soon you grow upset when a week has passed and you haven't heard from them. Repeatedly becoming emotionally upset over something like this comes from the ego, but the emotional sensitivities associated with the upset is a sign that you could have a higher probable degree of clairsentience, but it just it needs to be brought out and controlled.

The emotional upset experienced can also be a clairsentient message that this person is not as interested in you as you were hoping. They might be interested in you on some level, but not in the way you crave. Deep down you know this to be true since it came through your clairsentience psychic sense, but your ego is reactive because it's not what you want. This is also an example of the tug of war between the ego and the psychic sense part of you. To endure keeping this connection alive would only frustrate and depress you. When they give you a rare 'like' or comment on your social media page, or they text you, then this catapults you into feeling as if this person is deeply interested in you. The truth may be they like you on some level, but not in the deep way you're craving.

Pay attention to your feelings since this can be an accurate barometer gauge on what is real and what is not. When you move your ego out of the way, then you're able to decipher the accuracy of Heaven's incoming messages through clairsentience.

Someone with clairsentience can be all over the place when it comes to feelings and emotions. You will want to ensure you work on well-being exercises that keep your emotional balance on an equal footing in order to communicate with Heaven efficiently. With clairvoyance, the clairvoyant will hear someone telling them a story and will see the story as if it were a movie and actually happening to them. With clairsentience, the person listening to the story will 'feel' what's happening in the story as if it's happening to them. Sometimes if it's a horrific story the clairsentient may say, "You have to stop."

This is because the feelings they're experiencing over the story are so overwhelming it's as if it's happening to them. Clairsentience beings can feel things deeper than most.

Gifted actors tend to have highly calibrated clairsentience clair channels, which enable them to effectively inhabit a character as if they're walking in that person's shoes.

If others accuse you of always being too sensitive, then this is a clue that you may have a high degree of clairsentient gifts ready to be awakened. When others find you too sensitive, it can be because every little thing that someone says or does bothers you. Your ego is unable to control your reaction. When you develop your clairsentience and understand how it works, how to shield yourself, and put self-improvement into practice, then you react less to every shred that comes your way. You're able to manage it more efficiently over time with spiritual and emotional maturity.

When you have clairsentience, you receive hunches and gut feelings about situations and circumstances. You might have a gut feeling that you should've gone down one road, but you ignored that gut sense and went in the other direction where you find that a less than desirable circumstance takes place. Some have said, "I should've listened to that hunch I felt. And I knew what I was supposed to do, but I ignored it."

This is a sign that you're receiving guidance and messages from your Spirit team. Those with clairsentience absorb other people's energy like a sponge. They may find it difficult to be in overcrowded areas. They would be the ones that complain that it's challenging standing in a grocery store line due to the heavy input of other people's energies around them. The clairsentient can sense the emotions and feelings of others; therefore, they can intuit what someone is going through without words. At the same time, it can be psychic overload, which is why those with strong clairsentience keep to themselves or stay away from crowds or large amounts of people as much as possible.

Clairsentient people feel every little nuance around them to the point that it often becomes uncomfortable and draining. This prompts them to take frequent breaks of alone time. They'll be the one that leaves the party or event early as they can only handle people's energies in small doses. They sense everything around them from people's emotions to what's to come for someone. Their internal feelings are all over the place like a roller coaster ride every second. They might give the illusion they are extremely put together on the outside, but on the inside, they're wrestling with a roller coaster of emotions that constantly ebb and flow like the ocean. They could be prone to be a bit jumpy as if someone moved quickly behind them. They turn around to find no one there. Clairsentient people are ridden with anxiety, nervousness, and have a fight or flight response to any and all around them. Imagine absorbing everyone else's feelings being poured into you and how that might make you feel.

A clairsentient being feels the answers, messages, and guidance filtering through them from Heaven. The way Heaven communicates with this person is through their feeling sense. Someone that senses something specific has happened, is happening, or is going to happen is someone with a strong clairsentient psychic channel.

Clairaudience

Clairaudience means "Clear Hearing" (or Clear Audio). When you're clairaudient you hear the voices of God and your Spirit team. You can differentiate between the voices of you, your ego, and the voices of Spirit and Heaven by its accuracy of the message being relayed. Crazy voices are the ego or someone with an unbalanced mental health state pushing them to do something that isn't desirable such as harming someone. Spirit will never communicate to someone to hurt, hate, or harm anyone at all ever. They also won't advise someone on how to achieve fame or get rich quick schemes – things like that.

When you look back during the times you were in danger, you might recall when you received a heavenly message through your clairaudience channel. When there is an urgent situation that could put you in danger, you might hear a voice shout to you to run, which quickly gets you up and going. You later protest that if you didn't run who knows what might've happened.

Clairaudience is one of my dominate clairs where I hear voices, words, and sounds coming in through one of my ears that later comes true. Their voices are sometimes in unison or individually. The voices can sound disembodied or as if they're standing next to you. The voices are different than your own, but there may be cases when it might sound like you.

One of my ears is partially deaf, but the irony is that's the ear where spirits voices are crystal clear. I've been an avid music listener since I was a child, and I had pipe dreams of being a rocker or musician. I could live without communicating in any form except through the sounds of music. I hear the words clearly from my Spirit team as I'm listening to the notes and chord changes in a song. The words of Spirit flow and interweave through these notes effortlessly. My clairaudience channel works like an old radio where you're changing the station between the static to receive a clear station.

Every so often a ringing in my ear buzzes and

it's a sound that hasn't been detected to be a medical issue. This buzzing is the sound of my Spirit team downloading important information into my consciousness that is discovered to be of importance at a later date. The pattern was realized when every time the buzzing took place something of importance that comes to light psychically shows up in my consciousness afterwards. I've relayed messages to a stranger about someone that has passed on that they know, but who I don't. I've said their loved one's name as it is the name I hear through clairaudience. My psychic history has seemed to show that I nail names and time frames, which tend to be on the more challenging side to do. I wish I could offer some concrete instructions on how to do that, but I don't do any exercises. It's just always come in naturally even when I'm not trying to get anything.

Hearing things about others through clairaudience is what has convinced me that there is more to this life than this plane. I'm communicating with someone on the Other Side who I do not know. The stranger I'm relaying the information to informs me that it's someone they knew who passed away. There is no way I can know this information when it's a stranger, but they have confirmed that what I've told them is true. I hear the deceased person talking in my ear. They are not dead in the sense that one believes someone to be dead. They reside alive and well in a different plane than the Earthly plane. Having these occurrences happen sporadically throughout my life since I was old enough to construct sentences had convinced me early on that this is not the end.

Those with higher ranges of clairaudience tend to also be musicians and singers. They might not be aware of it, but they can certainly develop it. If someone's work is connected to sounds and music, then they hear guidance and messages through the notes of these sounds. Ludwig Van Beethoven composed some of the most memorable and beloved music in history, yet he was also considered deaf. This irony begged others to question, "How on Earth did he write these incredible pieces if he is deaf?"

His hearing was faint, but spirit infused his clairaudience channel with music that has long been remembered over the centuries.

Other clairaudients might find that they mumble or talk to themselves and yet they're perfectly sane. They are having conversations with spirit without realizing it or trying to. It's talking to someone the way you talk to a particular friend on the phone. The conversations or talking isn't random and full of gibberish. It is clear concise information that later proves true or is positively helpful to that person or another.

The voices a clairaudient hears are not to be mistaken with the voices that others hear instructing them to murder their Children or cause any other harm, hurt, or hate on someone else. They inaccurately claim the words come from God or that God is showing up in the form of that person. The voices of God, Heaven, and Spirit will never instruct someone to hate, harm, or hurt themselves or anyone else. Those are the voices of that person's ego, the Darkness, or Devil as some call it. The voices coming from God are always empowering, uplifting, and full of love even when warning of danger. These are traits that are the opposite of an individual claiming to be of God. Heaven instructs or offers messages and guidance that can help that individual or another person positively and with compassion. Those who are clairaudient will hear things that no one else can hear, which later come true.

Claircognizance

Claircognizance means "Clear Knowing" (or Clear Knowledge). Someone with claircognizance will receive messages and guidance from Heaven being dropped into their mind. They will typically announce something that they have no way of knowing only to find that it comes true. When asked how they know this information, they will be unable to efficiently answer that question. They have no idea how they came to receive this sudden insight. The messages sifted into their consciousness seemingly out of nowhere.

Someone might say, "You're absolutely right! How did you know that?"

You'll look at them stunned and say, "I don't know. It just came to me."

Those that have strong claircognizance are the bigger thinkers of the world that bring positive change, such as inventors, scientists, teachers, speakers, research investigators, and writers. These people are usually skeptical about where the information is coming from. Some of them might not believe in God or an afterlife. They need concrete evidence before they become a believer, but even then, they still function with some measure of uncertainty at times always looking for concrete tangible proof.

When someone exhibits claircognizance, they have the presence of being in control and in command. They always seem to have the answer for anything and everything that ends up assisting others in a positive way. Their mind is constantly turned on and in motion making mental lists that periodically come to them all day long throughout each day. When you receive a lightning bolt of an idea out of the blue that brings you positive success, then you can be assured that your claircognizant channel is functioning in top form.

Perhaps you're driving through a new town with a friend only to discover that you're both lost. You ask for heavenly assistance and you suddenly know to turn left up ahead. When you turn left you both find that you're no longer lost, and you know where you are. This is an example of receiving assistance through your claircognizant channel. It's receiving Divine guidance and inspiration into your consciousness that helps you know things that you didn't five minutes prior.

On another scale someone with deep claircognizance would be someone like Alexander Graham Bell's connection with the invention of the telephone or Thomas Edison and electricity. The information and data for those creations dropped into his consciousness.

Claircognizance is "knowing" the answer to something. You know what's coming up ahead or how something works. The information sifts into your consciousness from seemingly out of nowhere. This later proves true or is positively helpful to you or someone else.

Someone with claircognizance tends to tune everyone out unless it's a super important bullet point. They're the ones that interrupt others while in a conversation to bring their expertise or examples to what the person is talking about. They cannot help it as the information, guidance, and messages flows rapidly and effortlessly through the individual's claircognizance channel. This isn't to be confused with someone who interrupts others repeatedly for the sake of attention and to hear themselves talk, although many claircognizant people may do that. The messages the claircognizant picks up on come through with an underlying tone of excitement. Suddenly the messenger cannot control themselves and needs to share it immediately. Claircognizant people might be called know-it-alls at one time or another, but that pun tends to come from those threatened by a different form of intelligence. While others find they want to listen to the claircognizant expand on certain topics, but it's often layered and detailed.

Someone with claircognizance may have difficulty sleeping as the thoughts in their mind never shut off. This isn't someone that has the occasional restless sleep over an issue that's happening to them personally, nor is it the restless sleep conjured up by a stressful time in your life. Claircognizant people are always tossing and turning from birth until human death, even when life is going great. Some of them may be prone to taking a sleeping pill, herbal relaxer, and even something harder at night. Otherwise their mind will never shut off and they'll never sleep.

Claircognizant people are always thinking and sometimes overthinking things in greater detail. Others tend to comment that they can see the claircognizant's mind wheels always churning. The claircognizant loves words and communication, whether that is being an avid writer, passionate reader, enthusiastic speaker, or all of the above. Musicians and singers are more apt to having clairaudience, but someone with claircognizance would be the songwriter of lyrics. The clairaudient would be the one jotting down the musical notes since they hear the sounds.

Because claircognizant people tend to have the right answers or know what to tell others that can assist that individual, this makes them the go to person whenever someone is having any kind of issue. It is rare for the claircognizant to go to anyone for advice, since they already tend to know the answers naturally. If they do go to someone else, then it's to compare the wisdom or get another point of view since they are a lifelong teacher and student type. They make excellent counselors, inventors, scientists, problem solvers, and writers.

Clairalience and Clairgustance

Clairalience means "Clear Smelling". Someone with clairalience smells scents that are not happening in real time or on this plane. You might suddenly smell Cedarwood and recall that this was the smell that your Grandmother used to have in her house. Yet, the smell is coming out of nowhere in the place where you currently live. This sudden scent around you that is not physically explainable can be that you're picking up on the presence of your Grandmother in the vicinity. She is communicating her presence through clairalience.

Clairgustance means "Clear Tasting". This is when you taste something seeping in from the spirit world. You can be lying in bed and suddenly you smell a foreign scent or taste chocolate and yet there is no rational place for the scent or taste to be coming from. You haven't eaten anything resembling chocolate and there are no smells burning anywhere near where you live that could resemble Cedarwood. These were a quick couple of examples of having clairalience or clairgustance.

Recap

All souls have built in psychic clair senses within them that allow spirit messages to flow to you sometimes without you realizing it.

Clairvoyance is the psychic information being projected to you through your Third Eye in between your physical eyes.

Clairsentience is the psychic information that comes through the feelings you get. I can receive a physical ailment on myself that ends up being someone around me that has that physical ailment.

Claircognizance is the psychic information coming through your sense of knowing. You just know something is going to happen or you know the information or answer without having been versed in it.

Clairaudience is the psychic information comes through an etheric voice speaking it to you. Anything that comes through your psychic senses would be something that ends up coming true. That would be the obvious key that it was a psychic hit and not your ego or the Darkness messing with you.

Every thought or feeling someone has is not a psychic hit or a mediumship dialogue from Spirit. Often, it's the mindless chatter of the ego. Therefore, being especially cognizant of what's going on in and around you can help you differentiate what is coming through is you, the ego, and lower self, as opposed to it being Divine psychic information or your higher self.

CHAPTER SIX

Picking Up on Heavenly Input

Heavenly guidance can come through as an answered prayer or a light bulb idea planted into your consciousness that causes you to leap with excitement and joy. This idea could be something geared towards one of your life purposes. One's life purpose is what benefits both you and others in some positive way. For instance, you make a million dollars that is Divinely guided to change your life from the dead end one that you've felt you've been in for years. The money isn't just to change your life, but it's to also give you more flexibility to be able to help others in some way. Helping others can be in donating of your time, compassion, and services. God knows that once you're taken care of and set up, then you're no longer living in the epicenter of the fear of not having security. You then have that extra time that you wasted living in that worry to become a blessing to others.

The ones that reach that success quicker are the ones that can squeeze in being of service or being a blessing to others while struggling in their own life. Because this also shows that your compassion is so great that you enjoy helping others when and where you can. Doing that also helps you be less-me focused in the worry about what you don't have. It gives you a break from that negative energy within you and into something more fulfilling by helping others.

Sometimes you make decisions that you believe to be heavenly guidance, but then you later get smacked down. It did not go as planned and you wonder if it was your ego that had pushed you to go after something instead of your Spirit team. You wonder and doubt whether you had accurately received heavenly messages and guidance. Your Spirit team may guide you to go after something, but then you find you fail at it. This is not a failure in the way you equate disappointment to be. You fall on your face after the first few tries, but you get up and climb back on that horse again. You learn more from failures than you do successes. Failure and struggle build character and gives you the tools that will become valuable when the achievement and success happens. You incorporate those lessons gained from the failures and apply them towards the success that comes about at a later date. Believe that you can do anything you want when you go after it with passion and persistence.

Developing a relationship with God and your Spirit team requires working with them regularly as you move along your life's path. They will show you the moves in life to take in steps. First, they show you the first step, you take that, and then they show you the next one and so forth. If someone takes years to pick up on the one step that's being relayed, then it will feel as if you're not moving. Your Spirit team is waiting for you to take that one step that they continuously implant into your consciousness in order to show you the next step. Often, I'll hear someone tell me that they're always thinking about doing this one thing, but they have yet to act on it. The fact that it's forever been in their mind for years is no accident. Sometimes the psychic information is sitting there in front of you, but you're not doing anything with it. This might be because you think it's your imagination and you're not aware that it's Divine guidance, or you may fear taking that step. They would never push you to take a step that they don't have complete confidence that you can do with amazing gusto. They psychically see you doing it and all going well, which is why they are guiding you to it. Your ego is getting in the way to delay you from making that move.

If you have trouble connecting with your guides, then stop what you're doing, including overthinking things. Move into a place of still calmness in order to get your soul centered. Take a few deep breaths if you need to relax. Take a stroll in nature somewhere to clear your mind. In that clear relaxed state, you are better able to pick up on the heavenly input of your Spirit team. The act of listening is to get in tune and receptive to the information, guidance, and messages being filtered through you from beyond.

You can practice the art of listening with those around you. If you take a step back and evaluate your behavior you can detect if you truly do listen to others or if you merely use them to vent and talk about your stuff. In order to better hear your Spirit team, practice listening in your everyday life. Strike up a conversation with a friend, acquaintance, family member, or stranger. Ask them questions so that the floor and spotlight belong to them. Sit back and listen to their response absorbing the words they're saying. Care about what they're telling you. Don't just listen to them talking while you figure out what you're going to say next. Care about each word they're saying and taking it in. This gets you into the practice of reducing your ego's plot to dominate, while getting your higher self to rise back up and listen and pay attention to the other person.

Listening is one of the most difficult things to do for people next to forgiveness. No one listens much anymore. Attention spans are short, and people are instantly reactive to what someone says or writes. This dominates rather than taking a moment to hear what someone is saying or read what someone is writing whether that's on a social media post, blog or book. This listening and paying attention exercise helps you to then pay more attention and listen to the guidance coming in from the Spirit world.

God and your Spirit team always communicate with you. No one is exempt from that, but the question is, "Are you listening?" When you talk excessively or cannot shut off the voices of your ego, then it can be difficult to pick up on what your Spirit team is trying to convey to you. Ironically you might notice that some that are unable to be less me-focus also tend to be non-believers of anything beyond the physical world.

Another exercise connected to listening and strengthening your psychic senses is to get into a quiet space at least once a day if you can. Turn off all distractions around you including cell phones and the television. If you live with other people, especially if they're making a ton of noise, then go into a room and close the door if possible or get out in nature. Close your windows briefly if you live on a street where you hear the noise of traffic, horns honking, loud talking, or sirens.

Play music by going for something ambient, chill-out, soft, or classical. Anything that is not loud and obtrusive. Adjust the volume level to one that is loud enough that it is not a distraction, or too low you can barely hear it. I love loud rock or classic rock music generally, but when I need to psychically connect or channel, then I change the music selection to something of an ambient, chillout, soft, light guitar or etheric nature. It is also brought down to a lower level. The repetitive consistency of the lower level type music also adjusts the neural activity or brain waves to that of relaxation, which is the gateway to opening the psychic channel connection with spirit. This is the frequency that allows the Divine messages to be easily picked up on.

Sit or lie down in a comfortable position and get relaxed so that you're brought into a calmer state of mind. Spirit messages are picked up on much easier when you're in a tranquil state. When you're stressed, busy, or have distractions going on, then those are blocks that prevent you from picking up on heavenly input. As you get relaxed it can take anywhere from five minutes or more depending on how easy or challenging it is for you to move into this calm state. When you are in this comfortable relaxed position, then there is room for God to come crashing in with your Spirit team.

Avoid straining to pick up on anything as that will block the input. Instead relax and allow the energy to flow through you naturally. Don't expect anything or try to push for messages or an answer. Remain in a content state where you are centered and not seeking anything out. You might do this several times and receive no Divine guidance. This doesn't mean they're ignoring you. Sometimes it can take practice getting yourself into a calm state numerous times before you start to receive a breakthrough.

Ask your Spirit team to show you signs that they're around you. The signs can be meticulously subtle, but when you're in tune to all that is around you outside of the physical world, then you pick up on the symbols effortlessly knowing without a doubt that it is a message. Second-guessing what you receive is generated by the lower self and ego.

Visualize a pathway out in nature that is winding up a grassy hill to two closed doors side by side next to one another. Watch the doors open gradually allowing in bright white light. This light is shining onto the focus of your dreams and desires. The doors are being pushed wide open. On the other side of that door are the moving images of what you desire. This is a canvas where you can allow your imagination to go wild in painting all the things you've ever wanted. This visualizing gets you in the habit of using your imagination more, which is also connected to the subconscious psychic part of your soul.

Work with your Spirit team by connecting with them regularly as if you would a close friend. Ask for regular guidance on the steps you need to take in order to obtain your dreams and desires. Ask Heaven for courage when you feel fear, or if you need a boost in faith when you experience doubt about something. Ask God if there is anything you need to know or a way that you can be of service. Solicit for supplies or additional income to put into your dreams if that's the purpose of connecting.

The basic action steps to do when you long for something is to pray, ask for help, listen, take action, put in positive energy and passion, and then believe it is here now. Combine those steps into a delicious cocktail of positive manifesting strength. Your psychic perception needs to be on the mark so that you can pick up on what you're receiving from spirit. Sometimes their response might come right away, while other times it might come in out of the blue long after you've connected.

When you are a fine-tuned well-oiled soul machine, then the communication line with your Spirit team grows to be effortless. They will nudge you to take the next step in going after what you want. They will let you know when to pull back or when to dive head on in. They see more than the human eye can fathom or comprehend. They have an airborne view of what's to come for you and they know when it's safe to proceed on, even if you are full of fear in taking that step, they know it's safe. You might ask for help with something, but then it doesn't come to pass. Sometimes you have to give it time. Months go by and suddenly what you asked for surfaces or a problem you had is resolved.

One way to tell if it's you or your guides communicating is that when you're talking, then you tend to hear or use the word, "I". It might be bathed in ego or negativity such as, "I'm not qualified to write about this topic."

When it's your Guide or Angel, then you will hear the word, "You". It will be immersed in love or optimism. This voice will say something like, "You will write about this topic as you are qualified more than you realize."

The voices of spirit operate on a high vibration and are filled with uplifting love that assists you or someone else in a positive way. The chatter in your ego mind causes confusion and chaos pushing you to act on those voices, which ends up bringing harm or disappointment. Voices from spirit are direct, optimistic, and filled with compassion and love even if it's sending you a warning.

The feeling of being trapped at times is another sign of one having higher psychic abilities. The trapped feeling is also the absorbing of the harsh energies being darted around this planet. You're absorbing it without intending to. This is someone with a higher degree of clairsentience.

Run psychic tests such as keeping a journal or notebook and record the information, messages, and guidance down that you think is your Spirit team. Revert to the notebook over time to see if what you wrote down ended up coming true or had a positive effect. If it did, then you know it was heavenly guidance. If it didn't, then that can also help in deciphering that it was your ego or an estimated guess. With continued practice, you notice when the guidance you pick up on is more on the mark or not.

CHAPTER SEVEN

Psychic Insights

Heaven and the Spirit World have an aerial of view of the trajectory of your life. They've informed me in the past that if human souls could see what they could see up ahead for them, then they wouldn't be complaining and whining so much. Every human soul can see much of what's up ahead for themselves through their own psychic foresight. Some have said they don't believe in psychic abilities, but they might believe that people can be intuitive. Being psychic or intuitive work hand in hand regardless of what you call it. You're tuning into your core psychic senses, which are communication receptors with worlds beyond this one. All souls have this ability to read better for themselves than anyone else can. Accurately reading for yourself or anyone can be challenging when your ego is ruling the show that is your life.

How often have you received an internal jolt that something was about to happen, and then it did? I've heard some non-believers take a step back and recall those rare incidents where the psychic phenomena that came in did indeed occur for them during a dire circumstance. Increasing the psychic frequency requires raising your vibration and tuning into what's outside of physical distractions. Putting trust and faith in God and your Spirit team helps in trusting the messages you receive. If you're experiencing an issue or you're longing for something to come about for you, then have patience and faith that what you desire will work out in your favor in the end. Take the higher view that the angels have which is to trust that what is to come about will on divine timing. Sometimes it's not what you predicted or what you hoped, but you learn to realize that how it turns out is often much better than you envisioned it to be in the end.

Heavenly psychic guidance sifts into your consciousness almost effortlessly while in a dreamlike meditative state. When you wake up from sleeping at night it's almost immediately that you may have forgotten your dream, even though you awoke from it minutes prior. This is what it's like before you enter an Earthly human life. Before you enter this life, your memory slate is wiped clean except for hints that include your life purpose. This is similar to your memory being wiped clean when you awaken from a profound dream. Only hints of this dream you had while sleeping are left if at all.

You made a contract with your Spirit team before you entered a human life. In this contract are things like the soul mates you would encounter, the things you would endure, your life purpose, when you will pass on and head back home. Some of what's also in the contract are the many challenges you are intended to endure for the purpose of soul growth. When your psychic prowess is running on high octane fuel, then the more information you can retrieve from this soul contract. Your memory is fully restored when you cross back over and head home into the next plane. Part of the role your Spirit team has with you is to help you fulfill elements of your soul contract. This is also why having a stronger psychic sense will help you in noticing when their guidance is coming in, because they are guiding you towards fulfilling the elements in your contract among other things.

Some live an entire Earthly life and do not fulfill their soul contract completely. They may not come to this realization until the final days on their death bed as a human soul. When they realize they are going to leave their physical body, then the reality and the fear might hit them at that point. They might say, "Why didn't I forgive him or her?" or "Why didn't I allow love in from this person?"

These words filter through your consciousness as you transition home to where you came from in the spirit world where your Spirit team and other members of your soul family greet you. What also takes place is going over your contract for that Earthly life you just came back from. You will be going over the entire life bit by bit. This consists of things such as what you did and what you didn't do. What you did to others and what others did to you. What you accomplished or neglected and so forth.

Let Go, Let God
Let Go, Let Flow

I receive some pretty common questions from readers. One of them is about love. People are frustrated about not being in a love relationship. The desperate need to have a lover is what blocks one from obtaining a lover. It's the negative feelings associated with that need, which includes the fear that it won't happen. When you let go of the negative desire and panic to obtain a lover, then the lover shows up. I can attest for me personally that this is true. Every serious love relationship I have been involved in throughout my entire life to date came to me and developed when I wasn't looking for anything. I was in a state of perfect contentment before it happened, and then it happened naturally. Part of working on spiritual evolvement is learning the nature of patience and tempering the ego. It is to trust God and the Universe to guide and glide you naturally towards your dreams. This isn't done in a reckless fury of a rush.

The second common question is surrounding one's career. Others are trying to figure out what type of career they want, or what job they should go after, and in what industry. The response my Spirit team gives me on that is to think about what your passion is beyond making money and then you have your answer. The desire to chase money as one's sole purpose will leave you dejected. I can also attest that the response to this question was accurate for me. I have never gone after a job or career position for the purpose of monetary gain. I went after it because I had a passion and desire for that type of work or position. The money wasn't on my radar. It ended up flowing in naturally and in great abundance more than expected. The increased financial flow for each work position I accepted in my life was the icing on the cake.

Pay attention to your senses when deciphering the incoming Heavenly guidance while on your life's journey. The guidance could come in the guises of déjà vu moments. Déjà vu moments can be psychic hits of the future or of the past. The past can be a previous life or someone else's past. This can be the case even though the déjà vu moment is playing out as if you're the main character.

The future psychically seen is what's to come, which also means it's not necessarily a vision of what's coming for you personally, but it can be someone's future around you. The way dreams and clairvoyant images come to you are not always direct. It may show you a vision, but one that is not necessarily going to play out exactly in the manner it's being displayed. Clairvoyant hits sometimes need to be decoded and interpreted.

Sometimes another person's guides will communicate with my guides. My guides will then interpret what the other person's guides are relaying. They communicate at a fast pace that it overlaps with one another. It's much different in communicating than the way we do here on Earth in the physical body.

Obtaining a Psychic Reading

Since all souls are born with measuring psychic gifts, this means you can also all train yourself to pay attention to the input you receive. It takes work to strip away the materialistic desires that dominate in life so that you can be a stronger psychic vessel. This doesn't mean you can't desire physical needs, but it's not dominating or burdening you. With practice and work, you can be just as capable of giving and receiving reads for yourself as a professional psychic reader can.

Professional psychic readers or mediums find it difficult to read for themselves, since their judgment is clouded and not objective. This is why many will read with another reader from someone that is not emotionally invested in their life. This is also why many psychics do not read for friends or people they know since it becomes a conflict of interest and can taint the reading. They have emotion invested in their friend and may bend the read to favor the friend. In the end a false read is given, and the friend is not helped. Sometimes it causes the ending of a friendship where the friend feels uncomfortable by what their psychic reader friend has relayed to them.

Searching for the right psychic reader can be challenging and much like searching for the right Doctor. Readers read in a variety of ways. Some are tarot or angel card readers, some are fortune tellers, others channel messages from the Other Side, and some use objects, while others use nothing, but their own soul as the divination tool. There will be a synastry between you and the reader that feels comfortable for you both. No reader should tell you what to do. For example, they should never instruct you to leave a lover unless the lover is abusive. The role of an ethical reader is to simply guide or inform you of what they are seeing about a person or situation in question. They should remain completely objective and neutral in your situation. This is how your guide or angel is with you. They are guiding you and not telling you what to do. They are giving you free will choice as an independent soul to make the right decision.

An ethical reader would say something like, "If you stay with this person, then the philandering will continue. It is up to you to decide on your next course of action."

You have free will choice to decide what's best for you knowing this information. I've had angel reads, psychic reads, tarot reads, channel reads, and intuitive reads. I've witnessed those that use no divination tool, those who use boards, rocks or other devices. I love the craft and all points of view. I love watching and listening to the differing ways that others read. You gain different insights and perspectives with a different reader. It's a personal decision when choosing a reader to go with, just as you would in choosing a relationship. One person may love a reader that someone else did not gravitate towards. There is a synastry between reader and client.

Sometimes others that enjoy the psychic craft love to know what methods other reader's use when reading cards. I don't have a pattern that I stick with when reading and I rarely use any divination tools. I follow what my Spirit team is telling me through my soul and psychic clair sense channels. If there are moments when I need back up or want to double and triple confirm something, then I may pick up a deck.

I might then say while grabbing and shuffling the deck, "I want to know about a potential love for this person."

Nine times out of ten the card they have me flip over is the exact answer I had previously said without the card, but pulling the card gives my ego mind that additional confirmation needed.

Ask your guides and angels for clarity when you're puzzled by the information they're giving you. Request they show you signs and symbols to confirm what you're receiving from them. This is one way to determine if you're receiving accurate information or if it's your ego dominating the read. Every soul is born in tune to the Other Side and connected to God. The more a human soul allows their physical surroundings to influence them, the further away from God and heavenly communication you go.

It is also best to avoid volunteering psychic related information to others unless they've asked you for it. It's not particularly enjoyable watching someone head for a cliff and not being able to say anything. You cannot interfere with others free will choice. They must learn lessons on their own. I just keep it to myself unless I'm specifically asked if I'm seeing anything. If I'm asked what the best course of action is to take with a decision, then I'll let them know what I'm getting, but the answer needs to be prepared for. Often it may go through one ear out the other. They do the opposite, then come back to me to say, "Okay you were right, now what do I do? How do I get out of this?"

It's uncomfortable to not come off as if you're shattering someone's dreams. I'm all for one going after what they want. They're excited about something and you do not want to crush that for them. You see it being a dead end or not ending well and they ask you about it. You have to be delicate in the delivery of what you're getting, while still allowing them their free will choice to make the ultimate decision while also being supportive too.

Is a Spirit Trying to Kill Me?

I've received common strange inquiries from others in the past where the person is saying that they're hearing voices, and the voices are saying they're going to kill them. You'd be surprised by some of the stuff that comes in. The inquiry comes to me wondering if it's a spirit on the Other Side.

When one is hearing harmful voices, then this is typically the voice of the ego. Spirits in Heaven communicate with love, while the Darkness and the ego communicates with hate and negativity. If it's a demon possession, they would take over your entire soul and body, but those cases are extremely rare despite how common it seems in Hollywood horror films.

The harmful spirits that reside in what some refer to as purgatory feed off a human soul's addictions. They may coax the human being to partake in an addiction. They don't have the kind of power to whisper they're going to kill that soul though. It would defeat their purpose as well since their goal is to get high through the human being's addiction or vice.

If you're hearing negative voices speaking to you, then you'll want to rule out some things. If you've had a traumatic experience in your life, then this can trigger up negative self-talk that might give one the impression it's a dangerous entity or spirit saying harmful negative things to you. Some post-traumatic stress side effects cause one's mind to splinter into different selves where it feels as if it's not you saying harmful things, but an entity or spirit. It can happen months or even years after the traumatic event. Most people have had at least one traumatic event or circumstance they can recall through the duration of their life that stands out. It could be something such as a love relationship breakup that left you wounded and depressed for a period of time or it can be an abusive situation you had to endure.

If the harmful voices are something that continues indefinitely, then it's best to seek out a mental health practitioner to adequately treat and/or diagnose the underlying cause. This can also rule out any deeper issues that might reside within you that need addressing and healing. The next step recommended is to go to a highly evolved healer, counselor, or therapist as you continue down your individual spiritual path. With practice you will be able to decipher what are your guides and angels, and when your ego mind is playing tricks on you such as with the voices.

CHAPTER EIGHT

Psychic Accuracy

It takes a great deal of work and practice to be able to detect when it's a psychic hit coming through compared to wishful thinking or a good guess. Grow to be hyper self-aware and conscious of everything in and around you. If someone fixates heavily on themselves with both the good and the bad, then this is a good start. You're already hyper intuitive about all facets of you that this can easily translate into being hyper intuitive to when it's your Spirit team communicating.

If repeated dark thoughts plague your mind, then examine your current well-being state. If one week you're suffering from raised depression or anxiety feelings, then the ominous thoughts can be ego based. You would need to rule other possibilities out such as what's going on in your physical life that could be causing it. Examine what foods, drinks, and supplements you're ingesting as that has an effect as well too. If you're on cloud nine and everything is great, then you get a random rush of something negative coming in, but it doesn't knock your current happy state of mind off balance, then it could likely be a psychic premonition.

A premonition or psychic hit typically continues to come into your consciousness repeatedly, whereas ego thoughts are all over the place, fear based, and inconsistent. If you receive a death feeling like you or someone else is going to die, then it doesn't necessarily mean an actual physical death is going to happen. It can be a circumstance coming into your life that might be challenging, either with you or someone around you. It can be a metaphysical death or the ending of one way of life. It can also indicate a major soul life transformation is about to take place, which can feel like a dark foreboding. It depends on numerous factors that include what the thought or feeling is, what and where your state of mind is at during the time of the thought or feeling, as well as other circumstances going on around you that could play a part.

Most fear-based thoughts that people have usually turn out to be untrue. Those types of feelings and thoughts come from the ego or the Darkness plaguing your aura into a state of instability. It wants to see you fail and will generate thoughts into your consciousness that are untrue. This can also be when someone is over worrying about something that ends up working out the way it's supposed to. Having an increased faith-based belief system engrained in the soul helps to calm your unstable nerves a bit more than those nerves would be without that belief system.

It's more than accepting or receiving a feeling or thought the instant it comes in. It's also paying attention to you and your surroundings to gauge how the information, guidance, and messages are coming into your psychic senses. You would also make note of what spiritual frequency you're operating at on that day. This requires hyper alertness and extreme discipline with your life and lifestyle choices. It takes constant daily work to become a strong healthy psychic vessel. It cannot be done for one week, then you get lazy a week later and then try to do it again two months later. You're basically starting all over when you put it off, so it is necessary to work on shifting your mindset to that of being an open psychic vessel. It's like taking certain vitamins or supplements where you must take them regularly to notice the positive benefits over time.

When it comes to beginning psychic development, many have informed me that they feel like they're making something up until the person they relayed the information to informs them that it ended up coming true. One key trait to remember is to trust. Trust what you're receiving from Spirit and don't worry if you're going to be wrong since that's a given. The psychic information may not mean anything to you, but it might mean something to someone else around you. If you're reading for someone else there's no reason to say, "This may be wrong, but I'm getting that..."

People already know you may be wrong, or it ends up not being true. There's no need to say that. The only times I've said something remotely close to that is when someone is upset by what I'm seeing, then I may say something like, "I hope I'm wrong for your sake."

Unfortunately, due to them being used to my accuracies, they fear that it is unlikely to be inaccurate. Clairvoyant hits will sometimes be brought to you through your dreams. It's your soul's job to decode the messages in your dreams. Jot down what happened in the dream before you forget it, then break up everything that was happening in the dream that you can remember and juxtapose this with what you're going through in your daily life at that time. It's a puzzle to put together to decipher what's being relayed to you from above. You could be getting a symbol or sign about something, but often psychic information is not exactly coming in the way one might think it means. You could get a symbol of a car, which might make one think they're going to buy a new car, but it can also be a road trip, an accident, or something else entirely with a car being the psychic clue. Sometimes there is no point or message in a dream. It's your subconscious projecting those images to you, while other times it is a Divine message.

There are people that can see symbols and signs if they have strong Clairvoyance, but even if they don't, they may see these things while in a lucid dreaming state. This is because the main part of your conscious is asleep, which helps in removing those lower self-sabotaging blocks that would prevent you from seeing a psychic related message while in a waking state. Those things some see that are like one another are real, but just in another plane seeping into this plane.

When you deliver spirit information to another person, keep in mind of what Heaven's set of appropriate code of etiquette guidelines are. It includes that you only state what you're being told by them to others in a way that is objective and compassionate. Say what you see, sense, know or hear, but avoid instructing the person what to do. Only go as far as to say, "If you do this, then this is what will happen."

If the other person says, "Which one should I do?"

The response should be, "That's up to you to decide."

Your friends or family might tell you what to do, but when you go to an objective psychic reader, then they should remain neutral. This includes never telling someone that their death or someone close to them is imminent.

Another psychic rule of etiquette is avoid entering someone's aura and giving them information unless they've expressed permission. Not doing that is similar to breaking into someone's house, which is an invasion of privacy. Especially don't do that to relay negative information. I heard one person that wasn't a practicing psychic telling people things like when their death is going to be, or not to drive because they're going to be getting into a major accident someday, and that there is a major Earthquake going to happen any day now. As many bad things as you can think of, this person was randomly telling people that. The people he was telling this to never asked him, it was randomly volunteered, and nor was he accurate anyway. The ego wants a new person to believe they're super psychic suddenly. This prompts them to runaround making outlandish uncalled for statements, which screams of inexperience and gives practicing or professional psychics a bad name.

An exception to this rule would be if you're friends with this person and you randomly blurt out things not realizing you're making a psychic statement. I've never personally blurted out something considered tragic like their death or a car accident. I keep those negative things to myself. I'm always moving cautiously and would never interrupt someone to say something off like, "I need to warn you, there is an airplane that's going to be hurled at your head next week. Avoid sitting on your living room couch."

Contrary to some storylines about psychics in Hollywood films, most psychic information that comes in are not big loud tragedies. The giveaway is if the person seems to recite that to everybody on top of not being asked permission for it.

Part of mediumship and psychic etiquette is that you are responsible when it comes to how you word or deliver information as much as possible. This also includes deciding whether it's your place to offer information. I've had some email me or my Editor to say that my Spirit Guides are trying to get my attention regarding an issue, so my guides are going through that person to tell me. My Editor said he's told people, "If his Spirit Guides are trying to relay a message to him, believe me he has no problem retrieving it on his own."

Approaching random people or messaging those you don't know to relay things like that is inappropriate human behavior, but it's also poor psychic etiquette. If you're bent on relaying psychic information, then ask the person if it would be okay if you psychically read them. If they say no, they don't want you entering their auric energy field, then move on. If they say yes, then carry on with the reading.

CHAPTER NINE

Psychic Timing

One of the soul lessons that all have in their contract is to learn the art of patience. Spirit isn't handing blessings to you as soon as you ask for it. They're not always going to relay psychic information to you if they know it is not time for it yet. They may also be prevented from revealing certain information too soon. If they were telling you everything all at once in one sitting, you wouldn't be able to retain all that information. And if you knew everything that was going to happen to you, then you would no longer live life. You might sit back, relax, and wait for the date that something is supposed to happen. Not doing anything is considered an action step in the eyes of the Universe. You are choosing not to do anything, which will block the circumstance from happening, which alters your souls' path. This is because you stopped doing anything subconsciously thinking this will land on your lap anyway, so you may as well do nothing.

If everyone were being handed blessings right away, then no one would learn anything. When I was sixteen years old, I knew I was going to work in the film business, but I didn't know when. Spirit Clairvoyantly showed me visuals of me in there and in that world. I knew it was coming, but I had no idea when exactly. All I knew was that it was on its way to happen soon. At the age of twenty-three, I received the lucky break call that changed my life and got me into the film business with one of the top five bankable movie stars at the time. This was seven years after the original psychic hits that were showing me in that world. The predicted psychic forecast eventually happened, but not as quickly as I thought.

If my Spirit team said I'd get it in three months and it didn't happen, then I'd be disappointed and let down, or I wouldn't have done anything to help move it along. Or if I demanded that I get in before that moment, and they gave me an opportunity, then the chances are the opportunity would have crashed and burned. Because I was forced to be patient and wait, the dream did come true and in more magnificent ways than I had ever imagined. It was so big that at that time people around me could not believe it. It was, "How-wha-how did you do this! This is impossible!" It was the same shock across the board because it was that major of a gig. Still to this day my entire film business tenure was bigger than what most long for in the business, especially for an average regular person such as myself with an abusive, poor background, and zero experience. This is said to illustrate that anything is possible to achieve regardless of where you came from.

Be patient for your dreams to come true. Know that if it's taking years to transpire that there could be other factors at play beyond your comprehension. Sometimes we must endure years of struggle before obtaining the gold. Because this builds character and makes you humble when it does come about. When you push for something to happen with frustration, then that pushes it further away. That impulsive energy creates a block that delays it from happening or pushes it further out in the distance.

Psychic timing is often impossible to predict, because there are numerous factors to consider that would delay something from taking place. It is true there have been occasions where I have predicted timing to the day. One thing to note is those were rare times when Spirit did give me a date through Clairaudience, and it happened on that date because no parties involved were delaying it through free will actions. Spirit doesn't usually offer exact timing in many cases. They might just say soon or further out in the distance. They might circle a general calendar date. If they say May 5th, it might not necessarily be on that day, but within or around the day. They might say May 5th and you wait around, but nothing happens so you figure it wasn't true. But then out of nowhere on July 18th is when what you were hoping for does happen. Time is fluid in the spirit world because they don't operate on the calendars that we do.

If I receive timing, then I'll say it out loud, but if I don't get any timing, then that just means I'm not being given timing for whatever reason. Sometimes forecasted predictions of what's to come are given by spirit on a need to know basis. There are times that even your Spirit team doesn't have the psychic answer to your question, because God is blocking it for them too. If it's blocked for them, then it's blocked for you. If they are exempt from knowing when something is to take place themselves, then they won't give timing. If they know when it'll happen, they will only say it if it has any benefit for the person.

Perhaps you've been waiting for years and have become discouraged to the point that you've stopped trying and given up on life. In that case if Spirit has the answer, then they will offer reassurance to the person that the event is indeed in the soul's contract to take place. Keep on believing, have faith, and remain patient. This is why sometimes you might have seen or heard others about to give up, but then a sliver of light shines in revealing some scattered mini blessings on the horizon, then this shakes that soul out of its rut motivating them to keep going. They are so grateful to have that tiny bit of blessing that popped in that it ignites their faith to believe something great is in the works. Those mini blessings dropped here and there also help in building humility into your character.

Sometimes God and Spirit need you to do your part. Many spend each day complaining that nothing good ever comes to help them. They lack motivation, passion, and drive. As a result, they ensure this state continues and so does God. Spirit is not about dropping blessings onto a soul that is stuck in sloth mode if the soul won't get up to put in somewhat of an effort. Putting in any effort repetitively prompts God to swoop in and start lighting more of the way. If you are paralyzed by fear, sadness, or any other negative emotion, then pray for help with that element first.

Other general reasons timing isn't given are that there are still circumstances that need to take place that will enlighten that person some more before what they want arrives. If it comes too soon before someone is ready, then it'll slip through that person's fingers because they weren't able to accept it in the right spirit, even if they think they are. What your ego believes and what God sees are two separate things.

Spirit is doing their best to make some of your wishes and dreams happen, but there are pieces within the puzzle that need to be maneuvered to orchestrate the circumstance to happen. It could be that Spirit is making it happen, such as they are bringing a certain soul mate person to you, but you both keep missing each other. One of you is not noticing the other one or you keep ignoring them. Neither of you are acting on it every time Spirit gets you in the room together.

Timing is fluid and non-existent in the spirit world. They have no concept of time because they don't operate on human made clocks. Timing is something human beings created because they function according to a clock. Timing is a foreign language to Spirit, even though they are aware we are operating by a clock created by us, but they don't care if their timing is not the same as your timing. We see things as a matter of racing against the clock, but they see it as an unimportant blip.

What if someone gives another person timing in a reading? What if that time frame predicted comes and nothing transpires as expected? One might assume the reader was off, wrong, or was being nice by giving them an estimated guess to satisfy the client. I've heard those stories, but then a year later the prediction comes true. Events took place that shifted the timing because Spirit cannot control the free will actions of human beings. They're not going to freely give timing to any reader, because Spirit doesn't care about the ego dramatics that human beings have where we want something now. They don't care about the ego's angry frustrated irritation. They will instead urge you to learn the lesson of patience.

One of the most demanding questions most often asked in a psychic read is, "When?" When will a circumstance happen? They want an exact date as to when they will meet that lover, start that new career, or buy that house. You're not on the phone with your plumber demanding to know when he's coming. You're talking to Spirit and they're not going to bow down to demanding questions like when. They have no qualms about ignoring that.

It is understandable that you want to know when something will happen, since you are in a human body and crave immediate material security. This physical comfort could come in the form of the great job, money, or awesome love for example. When these things don't seem to be forthcoming for a prolonged period, you might begin to grow permanently solemn, frustrated or disappointed. This state lowers your vibration, which could block or delay the event from taking place or push it further out until you've been made to be humble and accept where you are today first. This energy certainly doesn't bring the event to you quicker. It is always best to remain optimistic and cheerful when possible since that energy is what attracts in positive circumstances. This doesn't mean deny your low feelings, but to work on moving out of that and back into optimism through faith.

No psychic reader can necessarily predict when something is going to happen for someone anyway. Those in Heaven that relay information to the psychic conduit live in a world without devices such as calendars and clocks. There is no time that exists for Heaven in the way that human souls have made it on Earth. Therefore, it's near impossible for spirit guides and angels to give a psychic conduit an accurate time to give to their client as to when an event will take place. Time is fluid to those in the spirit world, so when they see a human soul wanting to know when something will take place, they will either ignore that or give their best estimated time frame if it is in their sphere of consciousness to give. Sometimes guides are also blocked from giving it.

Any time frame that happens to be given should be taken with a grain of salt. There are a great many factors that can and will often delay something from happening with any time frame predicted.

There are psychics that nail timing more times than not, but for the most part it's challenging to nail timing. You are gambling with someone's free will choice, which is unpredictable. I've nailed timing in the past and witnessed it happen later. I have had the person I've relayed the information to come back to me a year later. This was in order to say that something I stated a year ago has come true for them. When I used to offer professional readings and someone asked for timing on something, I would rarely relay it unless I heard a month or date slam into my psychic clairs during the read. The circumstances where I offered accurate timing were voluntarily on my part because my Spirit team happened to be highlighting a month, day or season through my clairaudience channel. I just included it as part of the read. If Spirit said nothing as to when something will happen, then I would just say, "I don't know. Soon."

There are reasons Spirit isn't telling you everything you're asking at that moment. Sometimes information is on a need to know basis. Your ego wants to know when something is going take place. Your higher self is not interested in the when or how, because it knows all is well and what is intended will be.

The timing that is given by a reader is the probable timing pending that you or other circumstances connected to your desire are not hindered by any of the party's free will. Free will is not taken seriously enough when it comes to psychic hits. Most human souls operate using free will choice. They rarely listen to their guides and angels. It is more about obtaining their desire immediately. For example, in a love read no one can predict the impulsive choices you or this potential lover might make on any given day. This alters what was originally predicted to happen.

There is a danger when a psychic gives someone a time frame as to when an event will happen. If the time frame the psychic gave comes and goes, then the one who was read for will debunk the psychic as being inaccurate or that it just isn't in the cards for them. Months or even years down the line it turns out that the event does eventually take place, but it is so far into the future that the client forgot all about the read to begin with.

One way to look at it is that a reader or your own guides and angels are informing you that something is indeed intended to happen. Don't worry yourself over the when and how it will happen. Otherwise you'll drive yourself into a mental obsession. This obsession is what lowers your vibration. When you are in a state of joy and contentment, in the here and now, then this raises your vibration. This then allows positive events to unfold, and even greater opportunities to reach you sooner than later.

I'm one of the most impatient people I know, so

this is something I can relate to. I know what it's like to want to know when something is going to take place and how frustrating it can be when time has gone by and nothing has come to pass. Heaven says to trust, have patience, and keep the faith. Know that the path you're on is the way it is for a reason. The choices you've previously made have led you to the place you're currently in. What you desire will reveal itself to you at just the right time. Speaking from personal experience, I can attest that this is true. Additionally, it's important to remember to follow the nudges, signs, and guidance that you're Spirit team are putting in front of you. If they are constantly dropping the same signs in front of you to go to a different part of town you normally go to, or another store that is off your typical route, then trust that. It could be they are trying to orchestrate something beneficial for you.

A psychic reader can rarely assist you with something like this. They might tell you that you're going to meet your next lover in October. October comes and goes, and you wonder why it never happened. Were you sitting around at home hiding out between the day of your psychic read and October? This makes it impossible for any lover to find you unless that soul mate rings your doorbell like the postman or delivery person.

When a psychic informs you about a probable situation coming up, then keep an open mind. Take steps that can help it come along to you more readily. If this is a love partner entering the picture, then this means get outside and mix with other people. Go out more often so that this wonderful lover can bump into you. Pay attention to your Spirit teams nudges on where to go if you're confused.

While out and about, if this potential lover approaches you and strikes up a friendly conversation, then let your guard down and throw on the charm with them. Smile, be engaging, warm and open. You might not be immediately aware that this person is the potential right away when they approach you. They might not be what you were originally envisioning or thought of, so you end up closing yourself off to someone that desires to engage with you in conversation.

Another important action step can be that it is you who will approach this lover instead of waiting for them to approach you. This is an easy step for an extroverted soul. If you're an introvert, then practice using your gifts of non-verbal telepathic communication on this potential. You can do this with a smile or by giving them a simple, "Hello." Pay attention to their body language and how responsive or unresponsive they are. This also means pay attention to your own body language. Do you stiffen up to a block of ice with an expressionless face when this person enters your vicinity and notices you, or do you smile back and acknowledge them?

This is a cold closed off world and some souls may have an automatic fight or flight response. They could be stunned that someone said hello to them let alone an attractive stranger. They might button up and turn away from you or give you a grunt of a response. Does that mean they're not interested? Not necessarily. When you're in tune to your surroundings, you can gauge whether someone is interested or not. Watch for the subtle cues in their body movement. Do they pull away from you feeling uninterested, angry or threatened? And do they suddenly soften and move back towards you with acknowledgment? Their movements may be subtle that you might not notice it right away. You assume they're not interested when they may either be shy or thrown off that someone good looking is engaging with them. Unless someone has been drinking in a bar to loosen up, most people are not used to others being nice to them, especially if you live in an overpopulated big city. If you're a woman, you might have a traditional way of believing how relationships should form. This is where you prefer the guy approaches you and strikes up a conversation. That was the way things once were, but times are significantly different. Now both men and women must do the work if they want to find a long-term loving relationship. If you're a woman, then you approach him with a hello.

If you're interested in a same sex love relationship, then you have additional factors that come into play or ones that might cross your mind. They might be things such as, "What if I approach this person and they don't go my way? Or what if they have a negative reaction to my sexuality?"

Of course, you would use precautions regardless of what your sexuality is when approaching a stranger. You're not going to blurt out: "Hey, I'm interested in you!"

This method could work, but being subtle and polite in your approach can go a long way. This is where you are striking up a conversation as if it were a potential friend. You'll eventually pick up on enough energy vibrations off the other person to determine what their interest level is. There are people that are super sociable and friendly. It doesn't mean they're necessarily seeing you as a potential lover.

Your Spirit team is not going to drop the great lover at your doorstep if you're hiding out at home and you never go out to mingle. They're not going to drop an awesome career opportunity in your life if you've never sent your resume or credentials out to potential employers. Heaven helps those that help themselves. They help those they see are taking action steps to try and make something happen. This is when they swoop in to meet you more than halfway. When you're passionate and positively driven and action oriented to achieve your desires, then it's that much quicker to arrive.

Spirit may see something coming soon, in the near future, or out in the distance. When Spirit says, "Coming soon", then that can be anywhere between next month to one year. "Far out in the future" would be beyond that from one year to several years or more. Some factors come into play such as free will choices that you or others make that can bend or extend the event you desire from happening, to when it was soul contracted to take place.

CHAPTER TEN

How Much Does
Your Spirit Team Know?

Common questions I hear from others are things such as, *"How does one explain horrendous rapes, murders, the torturing of innocent people, etc. Where were those people's guardian angels? You watch an episode of forensic files and it's enough to make you wonder. I wish there was an explanation that makes sense."*

It's an understandable concern with an answer that resides in plain view. It's not the job of God, a Spirit Guide, or a Guardian Angel to stop horrific acts from happening at the hands of a human being. Where in any soul contract does it indicate that this is the role they must play? They are guides, which means they guide. A guide's job is not to do things for you or stop things from taking place. There could be a variety of factors to dive deep into when considering why a tragic incident happens. One of them is that all souls including those in a human body are granted free will choice. They might be choosing to ignore the Divine guidance coming into their consciousness to stop them from conducting a harmful act on another person. It could be the victim brushed off nudges and warnings not to go to a certain place that day that ends up having a tragic occurrence.

Some survivors of a shooting for example have said that beforehand they felt like something was off and that they shouldn't be there. Other times Guides have orchestrated situations where authorities or other people are brought to light about a dangerous incident about to happen, but those people also ignored those warnings or found nothing fault worthy at the time of the investigation. Spirit can't do much else if people are not paying attention to them.

Many people on the planet either do not believe in Guides and Angels, or they are not paying attention to their Spirit team. This goes back to watching what you are ingesting in your body and make note of your state of mind, because all of that not only influences your physical body, but it also affects your connection with the Divine. If someone is mentally ill, they are not in their right mind to pick up on the messages and guidance coming in from above to stop any harm they plan on enacting. It's also presumptuous to assume that every shred of living and choices made by humankind can be or will be controlled by God and Spirit, while everyone kicks back and relaxes allowing them to control positive outcomes for you.

In a world plagued with mass shootings or terrorism, notice how a good deal of the events that were targeted were where it's crowded, with some being schools or businesses. Schools will typically run safety drills more often in the event of an emergency due to the rise in shootings. Many of the larger shootings have been in entertainment venues where alcohol is consumed. Alcohol dims and removes your tuned in connection with the Divine. No one is saying that you shouldn't drink or go to an entertainment establishment. This is something I've frequented and partaken in myself on occasion. The point is being aware that your Divine connection is dimmed to the point that you're not paying attention to your Spirit team's warnings that danger is near, so you need to be hyper vigilant and careful while out and about. Pay attention to everything and everyone around, while noting where the nearest exit is.

How often after these horrific traumatic events have taken place do you hear about a survivor explaining how they felt something was off before the tragedy, so they left the venue, and then the attack happened? That person was one of the few picking up on the Divine message warnings coming in. Crowded areas in general will create a block with the Divine because you're also picking up on other people's energies that cause psychic interference. This is partially why I avoid going to crowded places unless necessary or without choice. Many psychics, mediums, and sensitive intuitive empath's have also protested to having trouble going to places that are crowded as it messes with their sensitivities.

Some have asked how God can allow misfortunes happen to people. If you're on the freeway speeding and not paying attention to your Guide and Angel nudging you to slow down and pay attention, then there is only so much they can do to prevent an accident. This fate results in your death and other deaths based solely on your free will choice to act out in a way that is dangerous and detrimental.

A pilot of an airplane took down a plane and crashed it into a mountain with 144 passengers on it. When someone is at the helms of a manmade vessel with 144 lives in that one person's hands, then those passengers on the plane are under the rule of that one person. You might say those passengers did not deserve to die. Perhaps they prayed and no help was forthcoming. An aircraft is soaring in the Earth's atmosphere with someone operating on free will. They ignore any heavenly guidance that is dropped into their consciousness. Their Spirit team is doing whatever they possibly can to penetrate someone's state of consciousness. Those that chose to board the aircraft might have done so by free will choice. Perhaps their own team was nudging them to not get on the plane. Perhaps they made a prior agreement that this is how they would complete their Earthly life run. By the time they realized something wasn't right, it was too late to pray and ask for help. As stated, no heavenly spirit being can interfere on any human soul's free will choice, without an expressed invitation via mentally, out loud, or in prayer.

Part of the reason my Spirit team had me write the spiritual related books is to help people make positive choices in their life, which simultaneously improves your well-being. This is transferred to others around you when you lead by this example. You become a way shower, which touches one person, then another, and so forth. This work isn't effective in a sound bite in a social media meme to grow followers, or that gets liked, scrolled past, and discarded. It needs to be digested as an entire piece.

People that have attested to work on their well-being on all levels have purported to being more psychically in tune than they were before they did the work. The work is to arm those interested. That way when you've hit a wall of giving up, you're versed enough to take the inspirational words to heart and put them to good use to pull you back up quicker than if you didn't have them. Human life is governed by going through the motions. Go to work, the grocery store, pick up the kids, make dinner, and so on. There is little to no moments within our disciplined Earthly life routines to have just enough light open for God to come in.

More people than not are saturated into the physical material world. They have been trained by each other on how to function, behave, think, and what to go after in life. They are technologically based, which has its plusses, but the flip side is it blocks one from paying attention to any guidance being filtered into them from above. They operate on sound bites, blurbs, and the short and simple. In the cases where an accident has taken place, and someone that survived recalled feeling something foreboding beforehand, this was a clairsentience psychic hit they experienced. When a catastrophe or accident happens, it is also intended to act as a catalyst to wake humanity up from slumber to implement strategies that can prevent such a disaster from happening again.

How often do you sense something is about to happen and it does? Or you hear a voice inside you stating something that later comes true? You have free will choice to choose which path you would like to take, but choose wisely. Heading down the wrong path will result in a dead end or cause something catastrophic. The damaging effects of free will choice are showcased all around the world and in the media.

Some countries feed their children unhealthy diets, because it's all they know or it's all they can afford. Children are raised on these diets, and when they grow up, they raise their Children this way and so forth. This is the same with someone's values and beliefs. They gain that knowledge by how they were raised. It doesn't mean they're right, because it's all they know. The evolving or advanced souls are the ones that break away from that mold and realize there is something bigger than what they've been trained to know. They are aware they have a purpose here.

The Role of Spirit
is to Guide the Soul

You ask Heaven and your Spirit team for help and you receive. You ask people for help, and you may not receive. Others have protested to ask God for help, but nothing has come to fruition. They stop believing and their faith dwindles. If what you're asking for can only happen with the help of someone else, then you cannot blame Heaven when it doesn't happen.

Your Spirit team is the lineup of players in your life that reside on the Other Side in Heaven working with you and guiding you along your Earthly life path. They are made up of one Spirit Guide and one Guardian Angel. They are present with you when you are born into a life in the Earth plane. From that point on your journey, they remain with you until you meet up with them again when you pass on from this lifetime. If you are someone that works with Heaven, angels, guides, or any other benevolent beings, then you may have more than one guide and angel that come to your side. Some may stay with you permanently, while others will come in specifically during important junctures in your life and then leave once you have accomplished what needs to be done. In Football, your teammates are your family that have your back. This is the same way your Spirit team has your back and vice versa. You work together with one another as you are a family that has a relationship.

Let's say that you are spending your days longing for a romantic partner. If your Spirit Guide and Guardian Angel are working with you on other day-to-day situations, then you may have another guide or angel that joins you in your life assisting you on your search for the kind of soul mate that would be beneficial for you. This Spirit will work with your soul mates Spirit team in order to bring you two together.

You could be a busy professional and not active in the dating world aside from joining dating sites and dating apps to get to know potential suitors. Or perhaps you have done that, and it resulted in disappointment. This assigned "love guide" works with this other potential's guides to help you two to connect. You find you suddenly start crossing paths with the same person repeatedly at the store, at the gym, in an elevator, or even in a parking garage. There is a reason behind running into this same person consistently and randomly. You are attracted to them, and you notice they seem to be taking notice of you in a positive warm way, yet you both brush it off or do not act on it. This is partly due to your ego and partly how technology has trained others to communicate via technical devices, but rendered them incapable when face-to-face. Both of your Spirit team's will continue to work on getting you both together. It is up to the both of you to do the rest of the work. This work includes something that might be difficult for some such as saying hello.

If you find that every time you run into this person, the butterflies rise, you grow nervous, or feel inadequate, then mentally in prayer ask God and your Spirit team to help give you confidence and courage. What's the worst that is going to happen if you make a mistake by saying hello? The other person says nothing or reacts in a way that wasn't what you were expecting.

It is difficult for two people coming together today where primary means of communicating to each other is through technological devices. Now you're standing in front of someone and you're suddenly a mute. This other person is likely just as nervous as you. They might be kicking themselves for not responding adequately. If you continue to run into this person, you'll both grow more comfortable with the other one being around. It will get easier to begin conversation even if it's always *a hi, hello, how are you?* There are no missed opportunities. If the soul mate you are intended to connect with is meant to happen, then it will.

The "Free Will Universal Law" is God's law, which says that all souls have free will choice. God, Heaven, and any spirit being are not allowed to interfere or intervene with your free will choice, unless your free will choice is going to result in death before your time. And even in those instances your Spirit team is not always able to prevent premature death.

There are some that don't want to know the future. Some of the reasoning is due to fearing what might be seen, while others prefer to live life without interference of knowing what's supposed to happen. The other reasoning is some either don't believe in psychic foresight, or the opposite end of the spectrum is because one believes that wanting to know the future is demonic or is against God's law, which neither is true. Although, connecting with the Other Side can invite unwanted spirits if you're not careful. Ensure that you shield yourself with white protective light and invite in only the highest vibrational spirits.

Some have stated to being blocked from receiving spirit messages about what's to come for them, but it's not always a block that is the cause. There are answers to questions you're not intended to know either at that time or at all. If you are to know what's coming up ahead with something, then that information would continuously hit you repeatedly and indefinitely until you picked up on it or noticed it.

Spirit can counsel you about certain circumstances, but not if the outcome is also concealed from them too. If it's hidden from them, then it's unknown to you no matter how psychically gifted you are. You're also not intended to know what's coming as it will prevent you from doing the soul work that you need to do that will ultimately bring in what you're hoping will come to be for you. If you knew everything that was coming, then you wouldn't bother doing anything or putting in any work. You'd sit back and wait, which is a free will choice move that can prevent the outcome from taking place.

The job of a spirit guide is to guide, and not necessarily to inform you about every single detail on your path up ahead. The reasons as to why this is the case are wide and varied. There might be a test you must endure on your own without any handholding. They will not give you the answers to this test even if they are privy to those answers. This is the same way a teacher gives students a test in Earth schools. The teacher isn't going to give the student the answers, otherwise the student won't learn.

Spirit can and may guide you through certain circumstances, and put up warnings or hints if you were straying too far away from where you're supposed to be, but other than that it is up to you to make your own free will life choices. If everything was handed to you the second you asked for it, then you'd become spoiled, would never learn anything, and subsequently would not grow and evolve. When Children are handed everything, then they expect it and will become spoiled throwing a tantrum if they don't get it. The same goes for the soul.

There are certain circumstances preordained or predestined to one degree or another. This includes the many soul mates you cross paths with over the course of your life. Soul contracted circumstances could be missed out due to someone's free will choice. If two souls were intended to come together and unite, but one eventually denies that and moves away due to free will choice, then there is a backup plan where another soul mate will cross paths with you once the guides know for sure that the other soul mate will not be coming back. Spirit can see what's coming down the road towards you even if the soul mate is making poor life choices that prevent the union from happening. Spirit may see that the soul mate will still eventually wrap back around at a later date, but it's taking them longer to make it to you.

Spirit advises you in the areas Divinely allowed, while other times they must remain quiet for your soul's growth benefit. The more open you are, then the more in tune you are to pick up on the guidance they do have to offer. The higher your vibration, and the more in tune you are, then the more you're able to pick up and follow the guidance coming in. When you're in your mind or ego, you may rationalize, overthink, and compute information. When you're in your heart, then you can sense what the Divine is relaying. Your Divine psychic senses will tell you the truth.

If you were intended to know everything that was coming up ahead, then you wouldn't live life. You would instead kick back and do nothing since you already foresee what's coming. Therefore, what's relayed is on a need to know basis through spurts of information. If you're not picking up on anything surrounding an issue, then take that as a clue to continue living life and make sound choices to propel you forward. Spirit will jump in if it's something you're intended to know or that is okay for you to know at that time.

This is also the case if you're single and looking for a potential love partner. You may pick up on someone coming to you that may have dark hair, so you might stop searching for a potential partner, or you will push away the potential partner if they don't have the characteristics or statistics you were expecting. The psychic information you received could be incorrect and a fragment of your imagination. It could've been what your ego prefers, or your psychic hunch was semi-correct in that there is a person with dark hair coming in, but that's not the partner. That person could be the catalyst that sets up the meeting between you and the actual partner who ends up having light hair. Or the dark-haired person could have no connection to a potential partner at all and was simply a friend or acquaintance coming into the vicinity. You just psychically misread the person you received in visions.

In the end, when it comes to the right soul mate connection, then it will happen naturally. There will be no guessing or effort. You will both sense an instant attraction and camaraderie. You will also both take steps to connect mutually and without resistance or strong persuasion. The dance of the lights of both soul mate partners will intertwine effortlessly when they come together.

CHAPTER ELEVEN

Blocking Divine Guidance

Having a crystal-clear connection with Heaven requires a high vibration. You will know that state has been reached when you feel naturally uplifted, centered, focused, and clear minded. This means naturally and not through artificial substances, which often creates a block even though you're feeling high on life. Anyone buzzed on an alcoholic drink feels great, which is why some drink. It's why I used to drink like a fiend in my early twenties. It was to feel good since feeling good on my own wasn't working.

My Spirit team says the best way to achieve sharper psychic perception is by getting rid of anything humankind made. They understand this is not realistic or practical while having a human experience, but the closer you are to achieving that, then the greater the psychic communication line is.

Witness those who do not need much to survive, such as hermits or gypsies who live in nature solo. They live out in vast reservations of nature where Spirit's connection is strongest. It's positively valuable to take periodic bouts of time out or time off when possible to commune and meditate in nature. Take regular retreats when you can throughout each year. This means taking one to three days off at a time from your busy schedule when possible to vacation in a nature setting. This can be by visiting a beach, desert, ranch, lake, park, forest, or mountain area, unless you already live in a nature region. Avoid taking it for granted, since that can be easy to do until it's gone or taken away by life circumstance. Whenever I head down to my beach minutes away, I always feel this wave of feeling so blessed. I'm highly aware this is no accident.

If you're only able to do that one day a month, then that's better than not doing anything at all. Take a friend, your kids, a spouse, a neighbor, an acquaintance, a colleague, or lover if that will help motivate you to go. Sometimes when you make plans with someone else, it's more difficult to back out of it than if you were going alone. Some personalities prefer to go alone to clear the mind with no distractions at all.

Identifying Challenges and Blocks

One day you wake up and realize you suddenly don't like your job or the relationship you're in. Perhaps you no longer feel connected to some of your friends. If this feeling comes over you and never goes away, then this could be a likely sign that your soul is transforming and evolving. Your Spirit team may have instigated this progression to move you to the next plateau. They may see that many of the things in your life are causing major blocks with them, which simultaneously prevents larger blessings from coming into your life. You then begin to implement changes in your life that includes dissolving anything you see to be toxic.

Dissolving people or tougher circumstances can take time. Dissolving your job will be the hardest unless you're able to find another job immediately. You don't want to make any drastic reckless decisions such as quitting your job before you have another one. You certainly don't want to leave a love relationship abruptly, especially if it's not abusive in any form. Conversations with your partner should be had in explaining your newfound spiritual growth or personal changes you're experiencing that could be altering the dynamic of the relationship. You may even find that your partner is interested in it as well too, or at least accepting of it. Most everything is fixable in a relationship beyond the couple having immensely outgrown one another. The strongest exception is if you're in any kind of abusive connection, whether that is emotional, mental, or physical.

Take a good hard look at your life and examine every shred closely. You won't be able to do that in one day. Throughout different periods each week, your mind will drift towards parts of your life to do a thorough life review. This includes the things that are happening in the present as well as the past. Often the challenges one is having in the present are somehow related or connected to the past. This is whether it was a poor decision made in the past, or a challenging trait gained during your childhood or upbringing. You may not even realize that a traumatic event in your childhood made you gain fear traits that you ended up carrying with you throughout your adult life. This affects your current state today, since the karmic thread is connected to that time in your life. It will continue to be carried with you until acknowledgement over how it started came about. The next step is learning how to shed that part of you in order to be clear and free of its bindings.

There may be some things you participate in that you will not want to part with, but which are ultimately causing a block in your life. You are your own accurate barometer as to what changes you need to make. If you're unsure, then you'll have to continue living life until it comes to you. Ask for Divine assistance and help as to what needs to be released from your life, then pay attention to the signs coming in from above. This is not necessarily something that you'll come to the realization of in one day.

It can be days, weeks, or months before you realize, "A-ha! This is it. This is what was in my way. How did I not see this before?"

This is that magnificent moment of enlightenment and clarity. Other times, you may immediately know exactly what it is that needs to be changed in your life, and then you can begin working on removing it.

Sometimes your ego can deceive you into believing that you're not blocked by anything. An example would be the rush you receive from gossip or absorbing negative media that propels you to swim along with it. The rush is deceptive because it's also the same high you get from drugs, alcohol, food, or any other toxic vice. A toxic vice can be anything that ultimately contributes to your downfall whether physically, spiritually, mentally, or emotionally.

How about whenever you talk to a friend, then your body feels weak and worn out from them. Perhaps they seem to be patronizing, condescending or they make snide remarks whenever you say something. This is an example of a subtle toxic relationship, because they're not being overtly abusive. When you feel bothered by the call afterwards, then this is a sign that your vibration has dropped whenever you talk to this negative friend. They might be someone that always expresses anger, gossip, or complains. They could be consistently depressed, sad, and down in general without any interest of finding ways to move past that. No event makes them that way, but they are always in that state around the clock. This affects you, your vibration, and your overall state, because you are in that energy and you're absorbing it and becoming one with it.

It's one thing where you offer supportive action-oriented words that help this person move past it. It's another thing if they're just agreeing with you, but never taking action steps to correct this. They refuse to admit that their general demeanor has been on the negative side. Acknowledging your repetitive negative state is the same as awareness. Awareness is the first step on the path that leads to recovery. Much of the psychic blocks with the Divine that exist are throughout one's daily life including the people you connect with, work with, and get involved with.

Other examples of positive lifestyle changes that will raise your energy vibration to be a stronger psychic vessel are cleaning up your diet, eating healthier, breathing deeper, frequenting nature, and partaking in regular exercise. It is also avoiding large amounts of alcohol, drugs, the media, and people who are toxic, drowning in stress, depression, or poor life choices. This is not to say that you should abandon family members or loved ones that are under stress. There is a fine line between getting too involved that you fall into a dark hole with them or choosing to remain detached from their drama. You want to avoid being emotionally drawn into someone else's whirlwind of consistent upset, especially on a regular basis. It does nothing to help you and nor will it help by feeding them the same negative vibrational words they're exuding by agreeing with their chaos. This is like sprinkling lighter fluid on a burning fire. This energy expands causing more of that same substance. The hard-gritting practical world places huge heavy burdens on ones back that cuts off the psychic connection. Finding that healthy balance between both the grounded earth and the spiritual heaven is ideal.

Coffee and Alcohol Psychic Blocks

Your Spirit team is always communicating with you, but if you're not picking up on anything, then notice what you're consuming into your body that can be the culprit. What you ingest plays a part in what blocks the heavenly psychic connection line. This includes the foods and drinks you eat or drink, to the people you hang around with, to your lifestyle choices in general. Notice what feelings you're experiencing as a result of bringing any of this into your aura. If there are any negative based emotions within and around you afterwards, then that will influence the spirit communication line. If your thoughts are negative, judgmental, hyper critical, or full of fear, then that will also affect the psychic input. Everyone reacts differently to certain foods. One person can be fine with having a cup of coffee, while another person will be more sensitive to the stimuli it gives.

Many have asked if coffee and alcohol specifically blocks your psychic abilities. The short answer is yes to a degree for some folks, but the longer answer is that coffee and alcohol in large amounts significantly dims and blocks Divine communication. This is not necessarily the case if you have one cup of coffee, or one glass of wine, or one or two beers max occasionally. It's only when you start downing more than that where it can dim the communication line. This overloads your psychic system making it challenging to connect. This is an exercise each person will have to test out to see what works best. Test your connections with a cup of coffee and without one to see where you're most comfortable.

Coffee would also include products with caffeine content in it. Everyone's body chemistry is different where someone can have a cup of coffee or mild caffeine intake and it's not going to completely block the communication line, while others will receive a complete block. It's when you get into super high caffeine amounts causing your stress and anxiety levels to rise. It's the stress and anxiety feelings associated with it that dim or blocks the psychic communication line, and not necessarily the cup of coffee or glass of wine.

Not everyone experiences the same effects from caffeine or alcohol though. Someone can have a beer or two max and they find it awakens the connection line with the Other Side, yet the connection is short lived, because then you start coming down off the high within an hour or two later, and you feel groggy and lethargic. Your vibration starts to drop and the match between your high vibrational Spirit team grows further away, so with that said the buzz from alcohol is a temporary high like any sort of toxin.

When you get into three glasses of wine, or you're drinking a six-pack of beer, then you're in a drunken state and have no strong spirit connection. You might pick up on a word or two from God and your Spirit team, but anything coming in is garbled and unclear, or you simply receive nothing but silence. If you can't remember what you did or said drunk, then you're not going to recall anything from Spirit either. The bottom line is that if you receive silence and hear nothing, then you're experiencing a block. Something you've ingested has created this block, or it can be your emotional state is not on a high vibrational level, even though you might personally feel that you're fine. The clue is the silence you think you're getting from your Spirit team.

You might be under the impression God and your Spirit team is ignoring you, which is never true. It is you ignoring them through what you're absorbing into your aura. This is whether through your thoughts and emotions, to your food and drink intake. A drunken state will give you a complete block, partially because your mind is all over the place, scattered, in a fog, and unfocused. Drinking heavy alcohol until you're in a stupor will mess with this clear mindedness and drop your vibration.

This isn't telling anyone to quit drinking coffee, or caffeine, or alcohol, or bad foods, so don't misunderstand this to be a lecture or judgment. It's merely offering what can dim or block the communication line for those concerned. These are basic guidelines that you can consider or disregard if you choose.

As stated, everyone's physical and emotional

state is different from one another. Someone can have a beer or a cup of coffee and still have the connection, while someone else notices that it diminishes. I can have a beer or a glass of wine and pick up Spirit messages, but soon after as I come down or move into the buzzed phase is when I notice the connection begin to dim and disappear.

You may find that you love your daily glass of red wine, but one part of you wishes you didn't have that craving. You could decide to reduce the daily glass of red wine to several days a week instead of daily, then gradually move that to once a week, and then eventually to once in a blue moon. The once in a blue moon notion is where you can live without it, but once in a while you share some wine with a friend and you don't beat yourself up over it or feel guilt, since guilt feelings lowers your vibration too. You're able to keep your vices in moderation, but you're not quitting either unless you eventually choose.

It's sometimes easier to eliminate something when you gradually reduce the intake over a period rather than quitting cold turkey. This is because you're slowly and safely allowing yourself and your body to adjust to the new changes you're making. It's not as tough or challenging than if you stopped abruptly one day, which can cause withdrawals and side effects. This applies to anything you're longing to dissolve, reduce, or eliminate. We're just using the coffee and alcohol examples, but switch those words out to the vices you wish to change.

As you were reading those last few paragraphs, you likely already know what it is that has been a concern for you.

You know your body best when it comes to your intake of coffee, alcohol, red meat, dairy, etc. You know what you do, say, or think that will make you feel a certain way.

Like anything that can be damaging or toxic in large quantities, you want to keep the guilty pleasures in moderation if you have a passion for it to the point where you overindulge regularly to where you wind up face down on the floor all day accomplishing nothing towards building your dreams. This isn't for Spirit's benefit, but for your own well-being. They know that when you are vibrating at a higher level that you are more in tune to the guidance coming in that can help you achieve the dreams you long to conquer. It will also help in giving you more energy and focus to put towards doing other things you love.

I used to drink alcohol like a fiend in my early twenties, then one day as I moved into my mid-to-late twenties I changed. Those close to me noticed this drastic change.

It led to numerous questions darted my way, "How did you stop? Why did you stop?"

My initial response was, "I was tired of losing a day."

The misunderstanding was that I stopped and went completely abstinent, which is not true. I still have a beer or a glass of wine on rare occasions, but I'm no longer drinking a six pack or two bottles of wine in one sitting as I would do during my weekly party in a cup days throughout my late teens to early twenties. I felt like crap and would lose a day when I used to do that. I conducted a trial and error process where I discovered what would make me feel uncomfortable and lose my Spirit connection compared to what would strengthen my connection. I spent a great deal of my twenties and thirties keeping all of that to myself except to my circle of close ones. Eventually, I began sharing little reveals here and there through my writing work for those interested or curious in it. I would dissolve or eliminate certain toxic vices and pay attention to if I noticed any spiritual, emotional, or physical difference.

With coffee I discovered that it didn't seem to matter if I had a cup of coffee or not. This is because I felt the exact same way with or without it, so I would think, "Why am I drinking this every day? It's not doing anything of any benefit, since I still feel groggy afterwards."

This was my personal choice to work with my Spirit team to help dissolve my cravings. I'm not anti-coffee or anti-alcohol at all, but just no longer crave it anymore. Not that someone might not catch me have a fun coffee drink with a friend on a rare day, but mostly I stick with teas. You don't beat yourself up over breaking your little discipline routine once in a while. You're not going to go to Hell, and nor will you be banished out to pasture for enjoying a guilty pleasure from time to time.

Make note of what is a human made substance and what comes from the Earth. Human made substances tend to play a part in dimming the Spirit connection, while anything from the Earth can help enhance it such as fruits and vegetables. In the end, when you don't want to give up what you love or you're not ready, then remember the moderation rule if you're trying to simultaneously have a stronger Divine connection.

If you're going to conduct a psychic, angel, or spirit reading connection for yourself or someone else, then hold off on drinking those two margaritas until you're done. Hold off on eating a large meal as that can weigh you down and will reduce any heavenly communication. It is up to you to decide when you are ready to reduce, dissolve, or eliminate a toxin or block, and then begin that process safely with your Spirit team.

CHAPTER TWELVE

*Sensitivities are a Gift
from the Divine*

You might have a tougher time moving through the feelings associated with a Divine message if you're super sensitive. At the same time, the more sensitive you are, then the higher degree of clairsentience you have. It can be both a gift and a curse due to how emotions can make you feel. The trick is to use those emotions to your advantage. Mentally train yourself to view circumstance through emotional detachment so that the emotions don't drown and pull you under. Usually someone that picks up on psychic input regularly each day will be used to it, regardless if it's intense. If you watch the same scary movie repeatedly, then you jump less at the scare parts than you had done when you first watched the film.

Emotional detachment takes practice where you spend time working on how you comprehend situations around you and learning to not take much if anything personally. Let things that normally trigger you to roll off. It's re-training your mind on how it perceives circumstances whether in the physical or spirit worlds. This can be difficult for a sensitive, an empath, someone ridden with anxiety, or a Clairsentient, because it's their overall nature to feel the intense psychic input, the messages and guidance coming in, as well as other people's energies. Compounded onto that are day to day issues that happen in your physical life that can cause imbalance or upset.

As a clear sentient being, your goal is to gradually learn to not enter situations that you know will negatively tamper with your psyche. This includes avoiding locations you know will be crowded. You won't go to the mall or a grocery store in the middle of the day on a weekend. You'll avoid repetitively going to a gossip media site if you know it's going to upset your inner world on any level.

I have a Clairsentient friend that doesn't go outside until nighttime when most people are back indoors again. Although, in general he's a night owl and doesn't mind, but has said that he waits for people to go back inside so he can go outside without interference. There are occasions where this is an annoyance, but there is no wiser alternative that efficiently aligns with his equilibrium. You are making lifestyle adjustments that cause less aggravation on your emotional psychic system.

Whenever you arrive somewhere and see a crowd of people and feel dread or anxiety every single time, then this is a sign that you have strong Clairsentience. The extreme side of this fear manifests into social anxiety and/or agoraphobia, which can affect anyone regardless if you're shy or highly sociable.

I've come across people on both sides of the spectrum from the introverted to the extroverted that have Clairsentience. It's less shocking to find an introverted person with social anxiety or agoraphobia, but there are also extroverted people that crave constant social stimulation and are outgoing, but are also exceptionally sensitive that it keeps them tied to the home base unable to be out in crowds let alone outside in a busy place period. They have a harder time because part of their outgoing nature desires constant social engagement, yet the sensitive part of them causes them to take caution and retreat.

The psychic input coming in from Heaven doesn't typically bother me no matter how intense it is. This is because the input is usually surrounded with a layer of love. It's other people's energies that bother me, so I can't be around that no matter how desperately someone might want me to. I call on Archangel Michael to shield my soul with a layer of white holy light if I need to enter a nest of toxic energies on any given occasion.

Sometimes you can do everything possible to not be affected by psychic input and yet you're still affected. Mediums and psychics become used to the input over the course of their lifetime that they become less bothered by it, but it can still happen even for those that practice emotional detachment. There are times where I am jarred by the psychic input coming in, but it's a temporary jarring, and then it rolls off naturally on its own. It's not something I'm consciously aware I'm doing. If it's extreme, then it can take its toll on me energetically. In a sense, one can say it comes with the territory. Requesting regular assistance from Heaven helps ease the feelings. That means you ask them to shield you from any additional negative, toxic, and dark energy daily.

Pay Attention to Your Sensitivity

As a sensitive, you may find a tendency to take things darted at or around you personally. You might negatively react in ways that is disproportionate to the circumstance taking place. This is the case even if it doesn't feel that way. It is only in hindsight when you look back do you realize that there was something else going on with your feelings and state of mind that caused a larger reaction. It can be a challenge to decipher if what you're picking up on is a message from the Divine or from your ego. This challenge can span a lifetime as you learn to differentiate between all input you're picking up on, because it can come in at the same time, which will make it doubly confusing.

The good news is that because you're a sensitive, you are more in tune to the vibrations around you than others might be. It's just a matter of honing in on what is Heavenly guidance and what is not. The other plus is that if you're highly sensitive emotionally, then you feel the messages and guidance coming in from spirit. You are learning to distinguish between what is a Divine message and what is your lower-self yanking on the reigns. Your lower self is the space the darkness of your ego enjoys controlling and bringing out to cause chaos and turmoil. There is also the Darkness that exists in the spirit plane that some refer to as Hell. That Darkness has its minions attempting to infect human beings because it's so easy to do.

Learn to have a stronger relationship connection with your feelings, so that you can detect if an uneasy emotion is a psychic hit and heavenly guidance, a reaction from your ego, or a side effect from something you've ingested into your body. We know from the earlier chapter that too much caffeine can make you anxious and more stressed. Too much alcohol can cause you to feel erratic, angry, unsettled, or depressed. Some toxins you ingest can create artificial emotions that give the illusion that you're connected with spirit, when in truth you're connecting with your ego. Consuming toxins in large quantities can cause this deception, but again this is not condemning or judging anyone that indulges in it.

I have an extended family that enjoys their alcohol and weed and there is no judgment. I also have those friends that walk into my place, light up their weed vaporizer pen, and start blowing it out the window as if they're sipping water, so none of that bothers me. This is about being aware of what can cause some of the turmoil or disconnectedness with spirit. Keeping certain toxic guilty pleasures in check, balanced, and in moderation is harmless, but of course abstaining from the larger health harming toxins as much as possible is even better. You know what your guilty pleasures or vices are and whether it's hampering or enhancing your life in positive ways. The less you are on, the louder the voice of spirit is.

Being sensitive is a blessing from the Divine. You might not feel like it is when you're sensing every nuance within and around you, including the uncomfortable stuff. Pay attention to those sensations to determine whether it's your ego or Heaven relaying messages through your Clairsentient feeling sense. They could be guiding you to make lifestyle adjustments that continuously cause you turmoil. If the same person around you keeps instigating grief and upset, then what can you do to change that? If you've found a friend has pushed themselves into your life who you don't care for all that much, then what can you do about it? The immediate action step is to begin the process of dissolving them from your life or keep them at super low doses if you're not prepared for complete elimination. Sometimes it's not that simple if it's a spouse, parent, sibling, or close family member.

Think of you and your comfort before any other. It's not selfish to make sure you are taken care of first. Only when you're taken care of can you focus on others. Boundaries need to be set in your life where you are strict and disciplined about who and what you invite into your soul's auric home. These systematic restrictions also include what you're putting into your body.

What are you consuming that soon causes you to feel worse than you did before you consumed it? Sometimes the side effects are worse than the disease. Pay attention to what ultimately aggravates you and brings up negative feelings. You're more than likely a super sensitive being, so something will negatively affect your welfare more than it might with someone who is less sensitive. This includes who you surround yourself with, what you consume, and what you read, such as gossip or certain negative media. If your emotions are provoked into negativity whenever you read about the same topic, then stop seeking it out and reading it. Stop ingesting something that worsens your emotional state. Extricate someone out of your life that never brings anything positive to your world.

Pay attention to what you consume. If you're addicted to numerous daily energy drinks and you're always edgy and irritable, then it's time to dissolve or reduce the intake of this toxin. Seek out healthier alternatives that can help give you energy and focus without the side effects.

If you find you reach for a beer or a glass of wine after work every day and part of you desires to stop or it winds up making you feel worse, then rotate the days where you substitute the alcoholic drink one day and the next day you sit outside with a calming tea such as chamomile, lavender, or tension tamer tea.

Guilt feelings over anything will lower the soul's vibration and this includes feeling guilty over having a beer. If you're going to have the beer, then have it without guilt. The guilt emotions will reveal a drop in your vibration.

Three separate people take the same alternative herbal supplement only to discover they all had a different experience with it. Some had a positive experience, while another had negative side effects, and the third participant felt no noticeable change.

Someone says, "I have two beers and I don't feel much."

While another says, "I have one beer and I'm on the floor."

Everyone's physical chemistry is different from one another. What works for one person might not work for someone else. This is about knowing and understanding what you can safely handle by gauging the effects beforehand, during, and afterwards. This is all aligned with paying attention to everything within and around you. Awaken your extra sensory perception in all aspects of your life so that you may grow even more aware than you ever have.

Tune in and follow the guidance and leadership of God, Spirit, or Divine. Avoid allowing your purpose to be taken away by other people. They may not have malice by wanting you to follow them and do what they want you to do, but if that means it's going to take you down a path that is disagreeable to your soul, then you are going against your integrity and the repetitive warnings from your Spirit team that something is off. Spirit doesn't give you guidance and messages for their sake. They do it for your own protection and higher self's soul purpose. They can see what's coming up ahead even when you don't. You're not here to live other people's lives.

There may be times when you lose someone close to you by choosing not to do something that feels unfavorable to your heart. Your Spirit team has greater things in store for you beyond being held back by others. Avoid falling into the toxic allure of people pleasing. As a sensitive, you may be more caring and wanting to help, but if something feels off about what you're being asked to do, then trust that instinct. Generally, the first sense I receive about anything is often a psychic hit communicating something important that ends up coming to fruition. My personal guidance system comes from above, and not from other people, and so should yours. Your sensitivity is a gift to help you make the best decisions or course of action while on your life path, even if it's not what someone else wants you to do.

CHAPTER THIRTEEN

*Psychic Spirit Team Communication
and my Creative Channeling Process*

My Spirit team's perspective is different than
the outlook of the people living an Earthly
life, including myself at times. They give me
another angle to peer through in a sense. The way
I view things is split in parts. One of those parts is
that I have a human ego where I can become
affected over certain day to day practical things to a
degree as any other person. Although, I'm able to
take things more in stride and have it roll off with
the assistance and connection with my Spirit team.
Others around me have used the phrase, "Calm
inside the storm." They've said that while everyone
is running around creating or swirling around in
drama, I'm unaffected with unmoving rock like

strength.

In my earlier teen years, I wasn't working with my Spirit team daily the way I began to as I grew older, but I was in regular communication with them growing up only because it was inevitable. They have been communicating with me since I was a toddler. I don't remember when it started because it was as soon as I was conscious. They're communicating while I'm busy doing other things. I'm not connecting in the way it seems many connect, which is the candles, incense, and props. I can be walking to my car and I hear them informing me of something important. There was no way to run from it or not hear them in my world. The days I didn't work with them or I ignored them were highly noticeable. For instance, issues that popped up were more dramatic, heightened, intense, and all over the place. With Heaven's intervention, the issues were less intense and resolved quicker. I grew to learn they were trying to get my attention in order to work with them like any team would. I realized that I didn't need to go through life completely alone. You can call on them at any time, day or night, to help with something.

One other part of me is the consciousness of my Spirit team. This part of me has an emotionally detached aerial view of circumstances once the dark side of my ego and blocks are dissolved or reduced. Sometimes the answers Spirit gives me are not necessarily what one wants to hear. Nor are they answers that would give one peace of mind depending on how your ego takes it. There is a separation between who I am, and the spirit guidance offered. Falling into a channel for me when it comes to the work can happen naturally, effortlessly, and within seconds. It takes longer if I'm absorbed in someone else's drama, which I learned to avoid as I grew older. No matter how hard you try to dodge it, sometimes it lands on your lap for whatever reason, or you accidentally walk right into it carelessly.

The transition from the human part of me to my Spirit team happens within seconds. I might walk away giggling at some obscene practical joke I've played on someone and walk into the next room. I sit down and move both my hands over my crown and over my face mentally calling in my Spirit team and now I'm in the channeled connection. My Spirit team has the steering wheel and I'm in the passenger seat kicking back. There is an evident distinction between their helpful compassion to my personal crass extremism. I think some people expect me to be walking with my hands in the air connected every second. How odd would that look?

Heaven understands you're going through human experiences they cannot relate to since it is not the world they live in. They reside in a sphere of consciousness place that is all love, all knowing, uplifting joy, happiness, serenity, and peace. There is no antagonism, bullying, domination, and unkindness where they are. They view Earthly life behind a glass studying human behavior and actions like a therapist. They know the basis for life and the reasons things happen. They know the truth and reality that blindsides the ego. Even if the spirit in Heaven had once lived an Earthly life, they did during a time in Earth's history that is radically different than it is now. History and humanity are ever evolving at a slow pace, but it is evolving. It would progress much quicker if the darkness of ego were more accepting of other people. To not do so is naïve, animalistic, and primal.

You're having a human experience and with that there will be hurt, pain, and suffering. There are times where you unknowingly invited it in and other times when it was beyond your control due to free will.

The messages from Heaven come in clear and effortlessly when you are calm, peaceful, centered, and in an environment that matches those traits. Heavenly bliss is the state to thrive for and attain in order to access spirit information and guidance. The power of being in a nature locale is beyond measure. It's an impeccable location to connect with spirit or for a creative artist to create in. It's the space that the imagination reaches the channeling frequency that connects Spirit to human soul. Creative artists have a higher frequency of sensitivity that allows them to receive input from the Other Side, even if they're unaware this is where it's coming from. Messages and guidance filter in through your etheric senses, which are undetected by the physical part of you. It often sifts into your consciousness in a way that is not always clear. The information you receive can be discombobulated and all over the place depending on what state you're in.

My state of mind moves into a space where my consciousness is taken over by my Spirit team. When that happens, I have sudden volcanic energy bursts of messages flying in that I have to write out quickly before the moment is gone. The energy is fast paced and high that makes me feel like I can run a marathon. There is a small window before the door is shut again! Physical demands and life circumstances can play a part in that. I grow agitated if interrupted while in that high. This disruption is like being abruptly shaken awake from sleep in a frenzied force.

Once that natural high euphoria has reached its peak, my energy level suddenly and dramatically falls to the ground without warning, and so do the words. The communication door to Heaven has slammed shut and I'm no longer in the channel zone. I'm slumped over or on the floor trying to regain life force and energy to stand up. It can take a little while before I reach that state again, but I can get there quicker when I'm in a serene setting. Nature surroundings are a stronger environment to take a walk in afterwards. This is not as effective when you live in a noisy area that has too many people and cars. What also helps is going for a walk, jogging, hiking, or biking. Movement and physical activity are good to do no matter how much energy has been drained from the channeling session.

Mediums communicate with those that crossed over to the Other Side and relay messages to those on the Earth plane wanting to converse with their deceased loved one that reside in another plane.

Mediums are channeling, but channeling has a slightly differing goal than mediumship. Channelers will communicate information from more than one being or entity such as a team of Guides, whereas a Medium is connecting with a departed loved one in the spirit world. While psychics peer into the probable future by connecting with a guide or angel.

When I have the channeler hat on, then I communicate with a higher-level team of Spirit Guides, Guardian Angels, Saints, and Archangels primarily for the purpose of the work they have me do. The words in the work are intended to empower, inspire, and teach others that are interested or ready for the information. Sometimes one is guided to a book by their Spirit team because there might be one sentence you needed to read that is the answer to a question that has been up in the air for some time. I cannot articulate the messages efficiently through speaking. My mind moves too fast to verbalize it at times. It's easier for me to sit down and write it all out without distraction. It also comes out clearer pending my state of mind is free of toxins. Have you ever tried to email someone when you're upset? The email dictated comes out all wrong and nonsensical. You re-read it later and say, "Why did I send this?"

Describing how channeling works is like a gifted actor attempting to describe their process. Popular working actors have said they read the text on the page and interpret the words as best they can. Every actor has a different method and there is no right or wrong way. It is whatever works successfully for that person. This could be the same way that your psychic intuitive gifts might be stronger with Clairvoyance, but weaker with Claircognizance. Everyone's psychic gifts vary from one person to the next. Channeling works in this same fashion where other channelers communicate in a variety of different ways that are not similar to the way someone else does it.

I've been channeling naturally since I was a child, even though I never attributed a word to what I was doing. It was just a process that was taking place automatically the same way one speaks. It's not like they teach this stuff in school, although they should. People would be more connected and in tune, which would result in their life experiences being smoother and less troublesome. Those that want to thrive in the world of business, political, or legal arenas would be even more successful if they were psychically in tune.

When you fine tune your senses, then there is no telling what you can do. Creative people in the arts tend to be exceptional channelers. This includes musicians, singers, actors, artists, and writers. They have a strong measure of feeling able to walk in others shoes. They have a greater capacity of input in understanding all things beyond. They channel to write music, lyrics, books, and performing. This channeled information filters into them from above.

Some Mediums meditate to get into a trance like state. The reason this is an effective method is because you're taking at least a few minutes to quiet your mind. You're silencing everything around you in order to have a stronger connection with Spirit. When you quiet your thoughts and the noise of the outside world, then there is room for Spirit and God to come rushing in. Silencing everything is by removing any traces of negativity from your aura. If you're upset about something, then this will make it difficult to channel until you let that go and release it.

The connection comes and goes throughout the day depending on what my state of mind is like at any given moment. I'm an ever-flowing neurotic emotional mess, so when I'm moved into a state of reception, then the messages and guidance flows into my soul through one of my Clair channels and the connection is made. Asking for the connection to be made while in a meditative state doesn't always work for me since I operate on an adrenaline rush. Being in the channel, the connection smashes in without warning. The frequency brain waves move up and down on their own while I'm doing other things until there is a connection, then I stop and sit down to recite the information flowing in. It's almost like the tides of the ocean are constantly moving, and so is the frequency channel within my soul. If I'm disconnected at any moment, then that state can change three minutes later out of nowhere.

I will stare at a blank page of a potential manuscript for days and even weeks and then bam the channel connection is made. The information is either dictated to me clairaudiently, or it's all dumped into my mind in one sitting through claircognizance like a tidal wave gushing over land.

Sometimes they'll show me visuals through clairvoyance, while other times I'll feel it.

When I fall into the channel space for a project, then no interruptions are allowed. Breaking this rule interferes with the process and flow of input. Breaking away knocks me out of the channel momentum. It can destroy the creative process for the day. Once the Spirit connection is made during the creative process, then I separate and disappear for a while. This is also similar to the process of a working actor.

When I'm not channeling for the work, then day to day psychic hits are coming through sporadically via my Spirit team or council as I sometimes call them. As a child, I could hear voices of spirit communicating to me. Sometimes they spoke individually and other times in unison. I knew they weren't on this plane, but it felt like they were in the next room or standing next to me. I'd be outside playing, and I could hear them talking to me. At the time I never used the words guides, heaven, or Spirit team to describe them. When I was a child, I thought of them as people located somewhere else that wasn't on Earth. They have always been like a loving teaching counsel of souls, and yet they have always been right there with me travelling along wherever I went. I never thought of it as strange or different. They were never cruel and have always been kind and loving. I thought of them as my best friends outside of the physical human friendships. This is because they listened to me and heard my problems and offered assistance that helped me in some way. They knew and know everything about me, every secret, and every tiny shred of hidden nuances. They would tell me things that were about to happen and then it would come to light. It is the one area I have always felt truly loved unconditionally. In all the decades on this planet they have yet to utter one judgmental or condescending word, which is pretty miraculous considering that most people can't seem to get through one day without doing that. They have my back no matter what. When it's all you know, then you don't think twice about it. You gravitate more towards them and God over anything else without question or hesitation.

I assumed that everyone was communicating daily the way I was growing up, but I gradually discovered most were not paying much attention to their psychic senses. I later learned from my Spirit team that they could if they tuned in. My Spirit team had me go through tough tumultuous bootleg camp like exercises and struggles that showed me what would block the connection and what would open that connection.

All Souls Can Connect with the Divine

Some religious followers use their words to harm others or put people down and say that it is coming from God. While some non-believers will then retaliate and say that anyone who says their words are coming from God is a crazy person.

Both of those extreme points are false. God is everywhere. He is in every cell, atom, and ion that exists. He is the energy that makes up every centimeter on the planet, the universe, and all dimensions across time and space. He is within every human soul, animal, plant, you, and even the most harmful hate filled person. There is no escape from Him. You can refer to God to whatever sounds more comfortable to you like Spirit, the Light, the Universe, etc. The best parts of you are what God is and the worst parts are your ego, also known as the Devil or the Darkness. The only destruction and corruption going on in the world is done at the hands of humankind plagued and infected by that Darkness.

It doesn't matter what someone believes or does not believe, because He grants all living energy free will choice even if it's not true. The purpose for that is to help your soul learn, grow, and evolve. You don't learn, grow, and evolve unless you're granted the freedom to choose and experience things for yourself. You can stay stuck in a negative mindset or despise other people, but the only person it hurts in the end is you. It stunts your soul's growth even if you cannot see that it has at that moment. There is no clarity when the ego is running the show. At the end of your life run when you cross over, then the truth becomes clearer as you are shown images of all your human years on the planet and what you did or did not do with it. You're shown what you said or did not say to someone. This includes how that affected you and the other person, whether it was a loved one, or an acquaintance, or stranger. You experience those emotions through all perceptions.

Everyone is connected to God because there is no way you cannot be. It is easy to determine who is picking up on the voices of God and who is not. God has the highest vibration traits possible and imaginable. This means when you exude high vibration traits such as love, joy, and peace, then you are connected to God. When you exude traits that are the opposite of that such as hate, pain, negative feelings and thoughts, then you are disconnected from God. What this also means is that someone can be a practicing religious person who goes to Church regularly, but is a negative or mean person, then they are unaware they are disconnected from God in those moments.

You do not need to go into a Church to communicate with God. The media portrays cruel intentions born out of a religious person, so it gives all religious followers a bad name, but there are both good and bad people in every group that exists on the planet. You don't hear about the good, because the media consistently feeds you the negative. They dramatize stories because they know that's the only thing that can hook in the darkness of ego. One concludes that it must be all people in that group that are bad when that is all you hear.

An atheist or non-believer can be displaying compassionate, loving, and giving traits to others and IS connected to God more than they would believe. It doesn't matter if you go to Church every week and have crosses adorned all over your house.

If the actions you display are of a low vibration or negative, then you have no connection with God or your Spirit team in that moment.

I'm overtly sensitive to the point where it has been an issue in the practical world. It is that sensitivity gauge, which has enabled me to connect and communicate with a team of guides and angels as if one were pouring a glass of water or flicking on a light switch. Those that are equally sensitive and in tune understand this since it's something they experience as well. It is not limited to "special" people as every soul that exists is able to connect when they incorporate certain practices and lifestyle changes that enhance and awaken these gifts.

A practicing psychic has higher degrees of a Divine connection, because they participate in it regularly. When you do anything regularly, then you become better at it. As a high vibrational psychic vessel, you come to know to steer clear of drama, toxins, and negative people as much as possible. You're aware enough to know not to go to a busy grocery store at high noon on a weekend day if you can help it. You're not going to hang out on media sites or phone apps where harsh egoist words are darted at and around you.

I was able to successfully submerge myself into the practical world and function like any other material driven human being. Deep down I found the practical world jarring and those in it to be lacking compassion, soul, and heart. The dark side of humanity is aloof, cruel, abusive, and antagonistically self-absorbed. The only way to function in that nonsense and to get through it was to drown myself in addictions and distractions such as drugs, alcohol, cigarettes, and other time wasters. I discovered that these addictions also contributed to me being unable to fully hear the voices of Spirit. My Spirit team taught me that these addictions dimmed the communication channel to them.

Excellence is what I thrive for and I'm just as hard on myself as I am on anyone else. Part of this is my meticulous Virgo Rising. Like Heaven, they've shown me that human souls can go the distance and striving for excellence within and without if they have the passion and desire to.

Re-Center Yourself

The voices of spirit are uplifting and calm, even if it is warning you of danger. They will guide, inspire, and lovingly coax you onward on your higher self's path. Their intention is to help you stay focused and clear minded in order to accomplish your life purpose goals. They're not fans of seeing anyone experience negative emotions and therefore desire to help you swiftly move past that when it hits you. It's part of the human condition to have easy access to these feelings, since that is the doorway to communicating with Spirit. When the negative emotions overtake you, then this blocks communication and does more harm than good to your overall well-being.

Even the most centered person on the planet experiences negative feelings from time to time.

When that happens, they can readily glide over it and move back into a focused detached emotional state, rather than dwelling in the toxicity of negative emotions. Address something with assertive compassion that needs to be addressed, then let it go and move on.

The centered soul is in tune and can easily hone in on the reasoning behind someone's actions that might have bothered them to begin with. They do this without judgment. This isn't about making excuses for someone's poor behavior, but it's understanding what's behind an action and choosing not to be a part of any blame, drama, or anything that brings you down or negatively riles you up. When you move into negative territory, then revert to focusing on activities and people that make you smile. The clearer Divinely guided answers come in when you're centered and standing still.

Meditate, relax, and center yourself guru. Drink more water than usual to release the toxins accumulated in your organs, and in your emotional state as well. Things begin to feel good after you release the junk that clogs up your soul. It's healing, therapeutic, and freeing. When the Divinely guided answers come in, then allow it to flow into your consciousness.

Relaxing Exercise

Find a comfortable spot to sit and relax in. Breathe in deeply and exhale, then repeat breathing in and then out as you grow more relaxed. On every exhale, breathe out all traces of negativity. Breathe out any pain, hurt, or sadness you're holding inside. Breathe out all that toxic emotion. Breathe out elements of residual anger and any level or form of upset. Breathe out any envy, jealousy, doubts, and all hints of negative toxins and emotions.

Whenever you inhale, then in imagine you are breathing in the light. Drink in this light whenever you inhale. Allow the light to envelope you inside and out. Imagine it is diminishing and dissolving all lower energies. Allow it to blast away all remaining negativity in you. Breathe in and drink in this light. Exhale this light so that it is blown out of you and filling up your aura around your soul and body. Now you are bathing in this light inside and out. Every time you breathe, the light grows bigger and begins to sparkle. There is no escape from this light as it fills you up lifting you into a peaceful serene love and joyful feeling. Visualize and feel yourself being surrounded by this light of God lifting your vibration up. This is the space where psychic input comes flowing in. God did not make it difficult to connect with Spirit. It's a matter of relaxing and tuning in.

CHAPTER FOURTEEN

Spirit Guides and Angels

Your life force is the positive energy that flows through your soul. When it is operating at its highest state, then that is when you are most connected to God. When your life force energy drops, then this affects your mind and your physical body. This is followed by you experiencing a perpetual negative state, such as you're always getting sick, feeling depressed, or enduring a permanent stress state that never lightens. You lose interest in activities that once made you smile.

When your life force dwindles and remains permanently low, then it's time to ignite it. Igniting it will unleash any pent-up repression that might have been forced upon you at the hands of others or at your own doing. You are not moving through your life alone. Spirit helpers within reach are available the moment you call on them.

Your Guardian Angel is a spirit being who typically did not live a life as a human being, whereas your Spirit Guide has lived at least one Earthly life. Often your Spirit Guide is someone related to you. They can be a relative of yours from centuries ago or one who passed on not long before you were born. They go through formal training in Heaven before they can efficiently be allowed to guide an Earthly soul. One of the basic training rules given is they are not allowed to interfere with your free will choice unless it's to prevent your potential death before your time.

You might have more than one guide or angel if you are working with the Other Side and Heaven regularly. If you are involved in a life purpose activity that is geared towards assisting yourself or others on the planet in a positive way, then you may have more than one guide. Guides and Angels are also drawn to someone that displays love, joy, or peace traits on a regular basis. It can be someone that is innately a compassionate loving human being who does their best to do the right thing. This brightens that soul's light; which spirits see and feel. The guide or angel will come into that human soul's vicinity by being attracted to their light like a magnet.

If someone prays and communicates with God regularly, or works with spirit beings in Heaven, then they also tend to attract in other heavenly helpers to their side. These Guides and Angels might come into your space to begin the process of working with you in order to help you achieve a specific desire, pending that it is aligned with your higher self. They might come into your vicinity to work on easing your heart of sadness, anxiety, or stress brought upon by Earthly concerns and circumstances. You wake up one morning to discover that you're feeling quite good after experiencing a hard time. This is your Guardian Angel working on your spirit. You log onto the Internet and see an invitation to an event. You feel nudged to go to this event and while there you meet someone who becomes your love partner for life. This is your Spirit Guide working with you. Your Guardian Angel tends to focus on your thoughts and feeling state, while your Spirit Guide will focus on your external practical matters.

Your personal Spirit Guide and Guardian Angel will be among the mix of souls on the Other Side that greet you when you cross over and head back home. Some have referred to your team as your invisible helpers, but this is not entirely accurate since your Guide and Angel are not invisible. They might be hidden to the naked eye for many, but they are most definitely visible.

If you're someone with a highly calibrated psychic clair channels, then you're more apt to being aware of your Spirit team. Your team takes the form and shape that they know is familiar or comfortable for your human mind to process.

Others have been sharing their personal experiences and encounters with angels for centuries on all corners of the globe. The angels appear for that person just when they needed it most. Sometimes the angels materialize as a reminder to let you know they are indeed real and present for you. The angels and Archangels are God's hands and arms. They are an extension of Him. When you communicate with an angel, you are communicating with God. You are not praying to the angels, since all exaltation goes to God. Since it's difficult for a human soul to reach God, the angels are His gift to you in order to help you improve and raise your vibration so that your connection with Him is stronger. He is always communicating with you, but you do not pick up on that when experiencing any negative feelings. This is where the angels come in to lift you up so that you have a crystal-clear communication line with God.

My mother recalled a story when I was eight years old. We were walking through a mall making our way through one of the shops and I was lagging behind her out of curiosity. She noticed I stopped to study the statue figures of angels on a shelf. She watched me concerned because the look on my face was one of anger, as if someone had provoked me. I looked at her astonished and said with irritation, "Why are they all blonde with wings? That's not how they look."

Not all spirit beings have wings, and this includes angels, even though artists have been depicting angels with wings for eons. This is due to the light of the angel being so bright that it seems as if there are wings behind them. Angels appear how they want to for that specific person. Sometimes they appear as a human being that shows up to help you in some way, and then they vanish without a trace. Most angels typically appear with white and/or blue sparkling lights around them and through them. They are androgynous and not in human physical form, even though they may appear that way to ease the human mind.

One's Guide and Angel reside in the dimension above the Earth plane. It is easier to connect to them than if they were in one of the higher dimensions. Your Spirit team can see, hear, and feel you through this domain, but you will have a tougher time connecting with them in return due to the heavy density wall that separates these worlds.

There were episodes in the series *True Blood* that showcased a doorway into a fictionalized world where Fairies resided. The doorway and transporting part of that design was not far off from the transition of dimensions such as the Earth sphere to the next dimension where Heaven and the Realm world exist. Another Science Fiction piece that is also not far off in describing the spirit planes is the *Twilight Zone*. The logline of that series basically says that the twilight zone is the doorway into another dimension. The creators of these entertainment pieces and most Science Fiction entertainment come from one of the heavenly Realms where Star Souls are born (a.k.a. Star Child, Star Seed, Star Person). Some of the Star souls that have been born into a human body might not have been aware that they were receiving these visions, ideas, and information from above. Regardless, they've incorporated them into human reality. This information they receive is dropped into the deepest part of their consciousness. This subconscious space is where the connection with the Other Side resides.

You are a spirit whose life force never dies, even if it feels that way sometimes. Your spirit resides in a temporary physical body in order to have an Earthly life for a variety of purposes. The body you inhabit will not last forever. It will age and eventually give out. In the human reality, you call it a death, but it is not a true death since your spirit is still intact and alive. It is just no longer crammed and stuck in its human physical body that weighs you down. Your physical body is a rental and you want to take care of this rental with good diet and exercise. It is hoped that you won't trash it the way some trash their apartments.

In the spiritual genre, many use the terminology *Body, Mind and Soul.* Those affiliated with that genre have the goal of improving all aspects and the totality of oneself. This is by loving your body and taking care of it, but also by being aware that you have a soul that you need to take care of as well too. You want to be aware and in tune to the idea of who and what you are. When your physical body has given out and is no longer functioning, then your soul exits its body and passes through a tunnel of light to the Other Side. This Other Side is reached by moving through the doorway or tunnel of light into another dimension. This other dimension is where Heaven and other dimensions exist.

Often you agreed to have a physical life for a variety of purposes. Everyone is on the planet with the goal of spreading the three biggest traits aligned with God: Love, joy, and peace. All words affiliated with those three words describe what Heaven is like. You may look around and wonder how humanity grew to be removed from those phenomenal traits, but it is the reason you are here. Life is rough for some and reaching that state of being can be challenging, but it is not impossible.

Heaven cares about humanity and has been displeased with how everyone treats one another on Earth, not to mention the ongoing crises state the planet is in due to human tampering. This is from the environment, to the unnecessary destruction of nature, animals, and other people. Building physical dwellings on top of one another has contributed to this suffocating feeling and disconnected others from God. It's a struggle to reach a true connection with tampering energies around you, but alas it's not unmanageable with practice. Some are nonchalant and in denial about the current state of Earth. They debunk the idea that anything is wrong with it. They write it off and take no responsibility in contributing to the damage of the world.

Earthly life might sound like some kind of science experiment gone wild placing you here to live and then removing your memory of who and what you are. Your soul's memories are not completely erased, but just suppressed. The Earth's density and the many blocks around you have limited the important parts of this memory. Past life memories are reduced to nothing unless it is relevant. Otherwise you'd be experiencing heavy emotion over something you did in a past life.

All souls have access to the deeper parts of their consciousness. When you are born, you are completely psychic and in tune to all things around you, beyond, and on over to the Other Side. Gradually, your caregivers, peers, and the society you grew up in began to have a larger influence on your human development. They train you on what to like, what not to like, and how to think. The ones that break away from that cycle tend to be rapidly evolving souls. They know they have an important mission or purpose here, even if it's to spread compassion, love, or joy to others in some manner.

The negative influences around you dimmed your connection and light to Heaven. How these contributors did this was by putting images in front of you of the physical world and inflicting the limited routines onto your way of life that it became systematic. This included that you're disciplined and on a schedule. You go to bed at a certain hour and you wake up around the same hour. You have breakfast and you head off to school, or when you're older you head to a job or a career. The school schedule is relatively the same and so is your job schedule. You drive back and forth to work to make money to pay for your car, a place to live, food, as well as clothing. You do this for what feels like forever while falling deeper into the routine of physical Earthly life, which is not the soul's true existence at all in the end. This cycle continues indefinitely until you retire and wait to pass on. That will oppress any high vibrating soul if that's all it's doing. You need to physically survive and take care of yourself, but don't lose sight of who your soul is while on this journey.

If you do not feel you are psychically in tune, then your goal is to begin the process of becoming more in tune. This means paying attention to everything around you beyond the physical. None of that is real or important in the end. One thing that both believers and non-believers can agree upon is that one day this will all cease to exist for you. You will eventually depart this plane. There is no way around that, so why not make the most of it and raise your consciousness and do the soul work.

Your Guide and Angel assist and guide you down a path that benefits your higher self. Therefore, enhancing your psychic gifts is important. It's to be able to communicate with them more effortlessly. Your higher self is the part of your soul's consciousness that is aligned with optimism such as love, joy, and peace. These are words that are also what Heaven is like while living there. Your lower self is your ego and the part of you the Darkness does what it can to grow, since it loves seeing destruction and downfall. The Devil and Darkness are doing its job when you see humankind behaving at its worst. The Darkness is aligned with the harm, hurt, and hate traits. It is the bully that seeks to destroy someone else because they are different. It is the part of you that wallows in any negative feeling or thought. This might be anger, stress, depression, sadness, or confusion. Someone who is a gossip and trash talks others resides in their lower self. The lower self is cut off from God and is not psychic, while the higher self is part of God and the Holy Spirit. Your higher self is psychic and in tune with what resides beyond and outside of this physical existence.

You can call on your Spirit team any time. You can call on any higher being in heaven from someone you love that passed on, to other guides, angels, to God, to Jesus or whoever you feel closest to. You can also call on an Archangel. The Archangels are hierarchy spirit beings that manage the angels and reside in another dimension. Like Guides and Angels, you can request the assistance of a specific Archangel to come into your life when needed. Many of them have traits they specialize in, such as Archangel Michael is God's General. He goes to battle for you, gives you strength and courage, and protects you from harm. Archangel Raphael is the healing angel that can help with anything health or well-being related. He might assist by guiding you to exercise, change your diet, and find the right doctor, or healer. Archangel Gabriel helps the artists and parents of the world. She's the motivator pushing you to get to work on creative projects. Archangel Uriel is the one who gives you those great light bulb ideas and shines a light on the path you're intended to be on.

Like the angels, the Archangels are God's hands and arms, which means when you're communicating with an Archangel, you're immediately communing with God even if you're not intending to. Archangels, angels, and spirit guides show up in your vicinity the minute you call out to them.

CHAPTER FIFTEEN

You Are Psychic!

All souls are created equally and no one is more special than any other. A soul might incarnate into a human body on the Earth plane and appear visually different from another soul within its physical casing, but the soul itself is made up of the same substance as all souls. It incarnates into a human body to live an Earthly life with others who appear and act differently than they do. Part of the reason for this is in order to teach that soul to love and accept someone for their differences. If everyone appeared and acted the same, how boring would that be? Yet, that is what the ego desires. It wants everyone to look, act, and support the same things as it does or else there will be Hell to pay.

The planet would be a beautiful uplifting joyful place to be if every soul was operating from their true highest vibrational nature full time. Unfortunately, that is not realistic since the darkness of ego in humankind has made the planet a negative place to be living on. It turned Earth into a ticking time bomb on the fringes of exploding. It is a place ruled by greed, power, hatred, violence, and pain. Humankind is to blame for ensuring the planet remains in that negative state.

Obsessing over media stories will block your psychic radar. This applies to those who fall into the negative gossip about celebrity, entertainment, and politics. If you spend your days attacking political candidates or celebrities, then you have created a thick block between your Spirit team and your communication with them. When you consistently complain about a political candidate you don't like, or a celebrity you despise, or someone you don't support, then you have contributed to the negative energy state of the planet. Note the word *consistently*, meaning if you do it rarely such as once or twice, then it won't create that much of a dent, but multiply that with doing it regularly and with everyone else who is doing the same thing, and how often you're doing it, then you've got a disaster of toxic energy flooding the etheric atmosphere around Earth.

Are you a regular offender? Or did you allow it to slip out in conversation casually without malice a few times? The emotion behind the words adds weight to how large of a contribution it is. The more negative feeling the emotion is, then the more polluted the energy is being darted into the atmosphere. If you're communicating positive uplifting words about these things, then you are doing your part in uplifting the vibrational energy around the planet into that of love.

What did the cartoon character in the Disney film *Bambi* say? If you can't say anything nice, then don't say anything at all. It's as basic as that positive mantra that has been worded and re-worded over the centuries by those who desire others to be bathed in love and joy around the clock. They understand that being around a negative person just brings you down. Who wants to be around that? The ego does! The angels have joked that they are happy to mace anyone with white Light that is permanently stuck in the dark toxic cesspool of negativity, which is not a pleasant place to live.

Feeling any kind of negative emotion for a prolonged period will block Heavenly communication. This means if you're living under constant stress, heavily depressed, or perpetually angry. Those are the kinds of emotions that dim and block the communication line with the Other Side. This is also why working psychics and mediums typically take fifteen minutes or less before starting their readings for the day to relax, re-center, and turn the noise around them off. This way they can efficiently connect with the spirit worlds for accurate messages for that client.

You are a soul in a temporary human body with emotions, feelings, and thoughts you are wrestling with every second. Believe me I can relate having incarnated into a human family this lifetime with depression, anxiety, and suicidal tendencies right down my Mother's genetic line. I've battled depression, anxiety and negative thoughts on occasion just like any other. I'm not immune to falling down that rabbit hole, but I'm consciously aware of it and doing my best work to climb back out as quickly as possible because I know in the end it doesn't help me. I also know that it's not necessarily something that someone can control. It can take a lifetime of discipline battling mental disorders on this Earth plane. I've had lifelong anxiety and social anxiety over depression. The social anxiety was brought upon by an abusive childhood upbringing at the hands of a violent parent. The extreme social anxiety and anxiety symptoms were not present when I was born. They were engrained during my human development days. I understand what it's like to battle with mental disorders, but this isn't the same as falling into a perpetual pessimistic path about what's in the media. If I were a pessimist, I could never have accomplished the things I set out to do over the course of my life, even after numerous parties said I couldn't do it. I paid no mind and went after what I was intended to do and accomplished it. You can too!

A high vibrating soul can do their best to ensure they steer clear of drama by working hard to set up their life in a way that has minimal contact with the nonsense of physical life. The further you are away from the noise, then the stronger your psychic frequencies are.

The soul is a highly calibrated psychic machine that fluctuates up and down while inside the human body on the Earth plane. When it's in the spirit world it stays highly calibrated, but when on the Earth plane it bounces around all over the place due to the dense heavy thick atmosphere that surrounds the planet. Most of the particles that exist in this density is created by every soul on the planet by negative actions and thoughts. If the atmosphere is this extremely dense, then you can imagine how awful and toxic so many souls are in the way they act and think on a daily basis. It shouldn't be a surprise to anyone as to how bad it is, because all you have to do is log online to the Internet and skim gossip media sites and comments. Visit social media sites like Twitter, Instagram, or Facebook and you'll get a pretty good idea over how bad it is. The culprits and offenders are blind to the temporary rushed high they're wallowing in and are unaware they're doing anything wrong. It's the same way an abuser denies having abused anyone when an accusation is made. Holding a mirror up to oneself with objectiveness can help in seeing how bad one might be acting out. I've heard people tell others who act out, "You should watch yourself on video to see how bad you are with others. It might wake you up."

Luckily, there are many immensely awesome high vibrational light workers and warrior of lights who know their purpose and reason for incarnating during any time in history. They have chosen to steer clear of the drama and noise of the physical life and limit their posts and dealings to ones that are uplifting, empowering, and inspirational. They do their best to remain centered as much as possible in the eye of the hurricane.

Every soul has clairs (clear senses) and chakras (energy points) that move up and down and expand in and out. It acts like a gauge depending on where that soul's consciousness is at and what kind of emotions that soul is experiencing at any given moment during its existence. If you are riding sky high on love and joy, then your vibration raises. When your vibration raises, then so does your psychic antennae. If you are in the throes of any negative emotion, including complaining or whining about someone else, or what's being done to you, or how something upsets you, then this drops your vibration, and lowers your psychic frequency. It's just the way the soul is designed vibrating with varying colors and shades of the rainbow. It can glow a vibrant green color as it experiences healing, to an uplifting joyful bright yellow, to a purifying white, and then to the darkest shade of toxic black. This is all in the span of an hour depending on what that soul is experiencing in its life. If their emotions and moods fluctuate, then so does the psychic antennae.

It is the soul's goal to be aware of that and conscious of it. Knowing what will wear them down and what will enhance it. When you discover you've slipped into a low vibration, then work on raising your vibration again. Even the most compassionate loving person will slip into a low vibration. Sometimes it's not even at your own hands. You could be in line at a grocery store absorbing negative energies without realizing it, or you hear someone arguing with venom, or a friend darts gossip at you, or you read a negative post on social media, then your vibration begins to drop and you didn't intend for that to happen. You were minding your own business high on life and then the negative energies infiltrated you. When that happens, then work on re-raising your vibration, clearing your space, centering, and grounding yourself.

Over the centuries, it has been taught to believe that having psychic gifts are only for a select chosen few. The reality is that every soul is born with these gifts and capabilities of being a conduit with the Other Side, including the ones that are completely closed off and blocked to it. The more psychic hits you receive throughout the day will give you a clue as to when you are operating with a high vibration and when you're on a lower vibrational playing field. It is raising your vibration that gives one clearer psychic reception.

A Medium is someone that acts as a vessel of communication with the Other Side. Spirits on the Other Side live in a world that is high vibrational, which also means they have a high vibration. It's much easier to have a high vibration in the spirit world than it is in the practical world since the soul's natural state of being is high vibrational to begin with. The spirit world is bathed in high vibrational energy. There are no wars, hatred, anger, hating, or harming of any kind back home. It is 100% pure love, joy, and peace.

The spirit in Heaven has a high vibrational state of being and a human soul has a lower vibrational state even when operating at its highest potential. This can make the psychic connection challenging on Earth. This is also why even the best psychics will only receive pieces of information coming through that later prove to be accurate. They're not receiving the whole picture at times because their vibration is attempting to connect with the higher vibrational energy in the spirit world.

When the Medium wishes to make a stronger connection, they will work on raising their vibration to a higher state, and their Spirit team will begin to lower their vibration in order to reach the Medium. They are meeting the Medium conduit halfway, hence the word *Medium*, which is the halfway mark.

A Medium is psychic, but a psychic is not a Medium. Every soul is born psychic and has varying degrees of this ability, but that does not equate to being a Medium. A Medium communicates with spirits or those who have crossed over. They can gain broader access from the Other Side than a psychic can. While a psychic may receive random communication hits about the future, what's taken place, or is taking place. This is the basic difference between a psychic and Medium. Once you've awakened your psychic gifts, then it is easier to take that next step and make a spirit connection as a Medium.

Spirit helps by giving you what your soul needs in order to continue on its path. This means they don't necessarily give you what you want. There are reasons you are enduring challenges. While some of the challenges are at your ego's hand and by your own doing, other challenges are placed on your path for a reason that might include enlightening you in a way that helps you grow and evolve.

This is part of the reason a psychic can't give someone the winning lottery numbers. Naturally that would make someone's day especially those who are struggling financially. If Spirit gave billions of people on the planet the winning lottery numbers, then imagine what kind of disasters would come out of that. Spirit gives you what you need and not always what you want. The lottery numbers are computer generated and chosen through free will. Spirit is unable to override the free will choice of a human being unless it is to prevent their death before the time that was soul contracted.

In Heaven, all souls are of service balancing both work and play. This is what they desire of human souls who seem to do more work than play, or the opposite end of the spectrum more play and no work. They advise against primarily working without play because you'll experience burnout, and the flipside extreme of all play and no work, because then nothing gets accomplished. This also means even if they could, they wouldn't be passing out the winning lottery numbers to people anyway, especially to those souls who are not ready for it.

Having boundless money flowing in does not equate to happiness as there are a great many people who are financially well off and are still not happy or they are struggling in other areas.

While having enormous financial flow does help with the practical necessities required in life this is true, but it doesn't equate to being happy. You could achieve that and may possibly be happier than the drudgery of having to work at a job you despise, but if your soul isn't operating on a higher vibrational playing field, then misery sets in.

Spirit understands that human souls on Earth need money in order to survive on the planet. You primarily need clothes, food, and housing, but you desire love. Spirit will help each soul on the planet to ensure they are taken care of to the best that they can pending you invite them in to work with you since they cannot interfere in another soul's life unless specifically requested by that soul. They will guide you in action steps to take that will lead you closer to obtaining enough income to ensure you are living comfortably and at peace. This means guiding you to meaningful work that is aligned with your equilibrium. One that will make you happy to do. The cold structured 9-6 Monday thru Friday corporate world is not for everyone, and certainly not conducive to a sensitive soul. As it stands, Heavens view has been that the cold structured corporate worlds are in drastic need of re-structuring for morale alone. If you dread going into work each day, then you hate your job. This isn't healthy on your life force or souls' vibration. Some people are afraid to leave their job or try another one out, but sometimes taking a risk knowing that you have something to fall back on can get your energy flowing again.

Heaven also understands the need for law, order, structure, and discipline on Earth, otherwise there will be anarchy. There is a fine line between being too strict and not strict enough. Human rules and laws are enforced for a reason to keep the darkness of ego from acting out dangerously, which it's already doing. Imagine murders, rapes, severe crimes, huge theft, and vandalisms wreaking havoc and destroying Earth with no one to stop it, because human laws have been abolished, and there are no longer any law enforcement officers or a legal system in place to prevent or reduce it. The ones committing those types of dangerous heinous crimes would destroy the planet and each other in under a year.

This is also why many souls on the Other Side incarnate from realms that consist of Wise Ones and Knights. These are the task master rule making Earth Angels. And yes, of course it is true there are corrupted lower evolved souls in charge contributing to the noise. Yet, it's the calling of the Wise Ones and Knights to keep order to a degree. This also means that a lower evolved soul will not vibe well with a soul from those realms. Wise Ones tend to come off harsh at times and too much of a know-it-all that rubs the lower energies the wrong way. They are usually either extremely loved or extremely hated with little to no in between. The Knights have some compassion in there that tempers that harshness a bit.

You have psychic gifts that can assist yourself as well as others in a myriad of positive ways. When you tune into the vibrations from beyond and dissolve the blocks preventing the messages from coming in loud enough to grasp them, then you'll be amazed at what you pick up on. Everyone's methods of connecting with their Spirit team vary. You will discover along your journey as to what's working, what isn't, and how to navigate through that.

Through daily work, discipline, and exercises you can awaken your psychic sensitivity. It would require a lifestyle change as well as an open mind to seek out what might seem like the unknown, but it is truly home in reality to the soul. There are many avenues to take that can assist in cracking open your gifts, which are already built into each soul.

Spiritual studies have become widely accepted as the years have progressed. It's been a growing industry that incurs billions of dollars post 2000's. People are becoming more curious or interested in the genre and in wanting to gain knowledge surrounding this industry in order to help them reach a higher sense of peace.

It is true that some human souls seem to be much more in tune than others, but a great deal of that has to do with them diving into the craft regularly, and/or not allowing the practical world distractions to block them from peering through the veil efficiently.

There was a time in history that anyone believed to be psychic or a prophet, was a witch, Satan's helper, or sorcerer. They were condemned to death as a result. Even if you were considered different and set apart from society, then you were branded evil and were persecuted in some violent way. If you displayed those traits, then you were looked upon as the spawn of Satan and a blasphemous sinner. Many were killed for observing those traits either by beheading, hanging, strangulation, torturing, crucifixion, or by being burned or crushed to death. Times have significantly changed since those archaic days. Now more people are growing hip to the knowledge that all souls have these inherent God given gifts of Heavenly communication. Some are starting columns, blogs, You Tube video vlogs, social media sites, getting published, giving seminars, speeches, and on and on. Today it's celebrated when at one point in history it was shunned or forbidden. There is nothing sinful or forbidden about having a strong connection with Heaven in order to positively improve your life and the lives of others.

Even though the spiritual genre is becoming more celebrated or accepted, there are also a great many cases in some countries that have not progressed within the genre. They still observe the burning of people who seem to be *witches* during seemingly progressive times. One case involved a 20-year-old mother of two in Papua New Guinea. She was blamed for the death of a 6-year-old boy. A mob of relatives of the boy took the young mother and then stripped, tortured, and burned her alive. This was in 2013 and the world did not talk about it. How fast is Earth evolving away from that if this is still going on post 2000's? Perhaps in North America or in parts of Europe that is unheard of, but there are still some countries continuing to live in the stone ages. They need to be brought up to speed, but that isn't likely to happen soon. Earth has existed for centuries and yet exuding love seems to still be an impossible feat that many have no interest in. A book like this cannot be sold in some countries because of the content. This is what happens when a soul denies its true nature and refuses to educate itself, raise its consciousness, move forward and upward, and connect with the Divine.

The lower evolved look upon those set apart from the crowd as odd or weird, but those with a raised consciousness and a high vibration can see that person's greater purpose for standing out. If you are odd, then you are more gifted with a larger purpose than you can imagine. Following the crowd is playing it safe. Those considered odd or weird veer away from the norm because the norm needs to be changed.

While there has been a rise in atheism and anarchy as a side effect of the judgment that exists within organized religion, there has also been a rise of spiritualists professing to being psychically connected. This is no accident, because all souls are connected. If there is a soul energy living in an organism, plant, person, or animal, then it is psychically and energetically connected. You are also psychically and energetically connected to it too. Someone in tune to energies can hold a crystal or stone in their hand and sense the vibrations moving through it. They are aware of the movement taking place beyond the physical material life.

Psychics and Mediums who publicly profess to having a connection with the Other Side are simply recognizing the God given gifts within them that all are born with and that all can reach. One may not connect with the spirit world in the exact same way as another, but all souls have the capacity to have a strong connection with Spirit.

Track your interactions with your Guides and Angels by keeping a journal of the information you receive from above. Even if you think it might be your imagination, write it down anyway. Record each message you receive, whether you believe it's from your Spirit team, your ego, or your own intuition. After a month or a period of time has passed, then revert to it and jot down the outcome of that message. You will be able to tell the difference between the self-generated messages and the messages received from your guides. Trust the messages you receive without fear or doubt. If you make a mistake or you end up being wrong about something, big deal keep on going. Your ego will get in the way at times and create unnecessary negative self-talk that is not based in truth. Sometimes you make a mistake, but with practice you improve at focusing on what is your higher self and what is not.

Anyone can connect to the spirit world that works at it. You must take care of yourself on all levels, such as physically, spiritually, mentally, and emotionally. When you have raised your vibration on those key well-being traits, then the closer you are to receiving accurate, mind-blowing, heavenly communication.

Follow the strong black and white code of spiritual ethics as your gifts develop and expand. Avoid offering random serious psychic information to someone unless you've expressly asked them if it's okay to tap into their energy. While sometimes you may automatically be tapping into their energy without trying or intending to like myself, I avoid reaching out to someone or approaching them with dangerous challenging information unless specifically asked.

A good balanced diet helps to increase psychic awareness. This isn't a fun rule for some who love their guilty pleasures and believe me I understand as I have my own personal guilty pleasures, but I do keep it in moderation. It's human nature to be attracted to fun foods. The truth is that a good deal of these guilty pleasures dim or block the psychic input entirely. You are what you eat. This popular saying is true. If you continuously eat heavy foods that are not good for you, then that weighs you down. In order to assist in increasing psychic receptivity, you need healthy foods. These are foods that give you brain power and improve your health. Because when your body, mind, and soul are operating on high capacity, then this assists in increasing the awareness to spirit reception.

Your soul at its core is a high vibrational being filled with ever flowing love, joy, and serenity. Don't forget who you are. Don't get lost in the negative toxic energy of the physical world. Take care of yourself, which means taking care of your soul and body on all levels as much as possible. Incorporate healthy life changes you can make today that will help you in awakening the parts of you that existed from the conception of your soul. These are the parts that can help you be happier, stronger, and that much more powerful.

You were born a vessel of love! Even if you do nothing with the gifts that exist within you, you will at least be shining that bright light of high vibrational energy onto all those in your path, which in turn tempers the severity of the bullets firing all over the place by the darkness of ego. The ego may have tantrums and cause all sorts of noise, but contrary to belief, love is more powerful than any other energy that exists on any plane in the end. Let your love flow and shine outwardly wherever you go. Remember to revert to love, joy, and peace when possible. Take regular action steps that can help bring you back to this natural state of being whenever you falter on your path. Be conscious of who you are and the reservoir of gifts moving through you. This world needs more love and light in it. It is up to you to help guide others in that direction by doing the individual work to evolve and raise your consciousness. The planets ruler is not a human being. It is the Creator of all that is. Through the Divine is where effective positive change can happen within each individual.

CHAPTER SIXTEEN

How to Connect with the Tarot

When you're new to realizing the psychic gifts built within you, then you may at times doubt what you're picking up on wondering if it's really a psychic hit or not. One of the beneficial ways to knowing if you're receiving accurate Divinely guided psychic messages is to write down everything you're receiving. Keep a journal or an email folder that you record down anything you might consider to be a psychic message. This way you can go back to it months later or even years later to read through it to see if it was something that did come to fruition. Another way is to use a Divination tool. Divination tools have been used in the psychic field for centuries from using a pendulum, crystal ball, runes, angel board, tea leaves and so on. One of the most popular well-known divination tools is the Tarot.

I rarely use divination tools to connect with Spirit, but this doesn't mean I don't approve of it. I've been a Tarot enthusiast supporter, lover, and occasional user since I was a child. I remember being eight years old picking up my first Tarot card to look at it and suddenly messages were flying into my consciousness. I would then gaze at the dynamically stimulating images of the cards and allowing all the elements surrounding them to hit me like a tsunami wave. This is the same way I would sift through my parent's record collection fixating on the album covers when vinyl was the big thing. The images of the album covers were as vibrant and layered with detail as a Tarot card. Album covers are not as creative as they once used to be.

There are endless messages that can come through from staring at any image, let alone a Tarot card. If you have an attraction to art or a painting and find yourself picking up on what's unsaid and getting lost in the caverns of it, then you're that much closer to being able to efficiently and adequately read a Tarot card.

I've met CEO's that secretly admit to not making a decision without first connecting with the Tarot. Anyone can consult with the cards regardless of what position you hold in life. It doesn't matter if you're a lawyer, doctor, surfer, receptionist, garbage man, plumber, or politician. The Tarot is an exceptional communication device to receive messages, wisdom, and guidance from your Spirit team for any human soul on the planet.

The brilliance of the Tarot is that it's for anyone

who has a passion for the cards. You don't have to be a professional psychic or medium to use the tool. There are endless varying takes of the meanings of Tarot cards in a reading that one tried or true way doesn't exist. When you feel confident enough with the cards, then you'll have your own methods that work.

I've always found the Tarot to be an excellent divination tool from which to confirm messages with my own Spirit team whenever I felt the incoming messages to be hazy or unclear. Spirit would then guide me to the right Tarot card to flip over so I could see or confirm what they wanted me to know through a card. Spirit communicates through symbols and signs as well as other means that can get your attention. Since the Tarot is ripe with symbolism, this is a great way for them to relay messages to you. Diving into the worlds of the Tarot can take a lifetime of endless study. When you enjoy what you're immersing yourself into, then it ends up being a gratifying experience.

How I Connect with the Tarot

My Spirit team has been communicating with me through my etheric clair channels throughout the course of my entire life. Everyone has this ability since these etheric channels reside within all souls. The unseen senses are one of the many ways that Spirit can communicate with you. My soul, mind, and body has been an extraordinary vessel of psychic communication without the use of any other device.

This is a physical world with an enormous coating of thick density that acts as a wall between this world and the next. Earthly distractions, erratic emotions, and physical pleasures can block or dim the communication line with Spirit. There might be moments when your vibration is not as high as it could be. The Divine messages coming through are not loud enough, or your ego steps in to second guess what's relayed. This is where the Tarot or any Oracle for that matter can be of benefit.

The Tarot is an extension of myself when seeking to expand or confirm what's coming through. I throw down a card and flip it over only to find that the message is the one my Spirit team had informed me about. I use the Tarot partially to confirm information I'm picking up on and because it's fun to play with. It's like someone that loves playing Blackjack or any other fun card games. I find the Tarot equally enjoyable and entertaining. It is also a way for me to have a phone call with my Spirit team when the supplementary ways they communicate are not coming in clear enough. This is no different than what anyone can do when you tune in to everything that is outside of the physical concrete world that distracts you.

Your Spirit team is communicating with you daily whether you are aware of it or not. They will communicate with you through one or more of your clair channels. Pay attention to your clair senses in order to pick up on the messages and guidance filtering through you from God, a higher power, your higher self, universe, heaven, your guides, angels, or whoever you're comfortable with calling it. In the end, the messages and guidance are coming in from beyond the physical materialistic distracting world known as the Earthly life.

Having crystal clear communication with your Spirit team can assist you with your Tarot readings. Tarot is an exceptional divination tool to help you in picking up on what is being relayed. This is especially helpful if your psychic clair channels have dimmed, you're second guessing the guidance, or you feel you're not picking up on anything.

I've been reading with hundreds of people since I was a teenager as I enjoy the psychic craft. I've unsurprisingly also made many additional friends in the Tarot reading world as a result. I love watching how others read since each way one reads is varying. Every single reader reads differently from one another. There are no two people who read the same way. This is because everyone has varying gifts in the way they interpret messages from the Other Side. If one reader doesn't work for you, then there will be a reader who does. This also means that you likely read and interpret differently than others do.

It is often advised that you avoid reading for yourself. This is because you may unknowingly taint your reading by bending it to suit what you're desiring. This won't stop anyone from reading for themselves, but take precaution by being as objective as possible when you do.

Avoid reading for yourself or for anyone when you're not in a state of complete open psychic reception. This means if you're emotionally upset, angry, depressed, or any other negative emotion, then this can fault the reading. The same goes if you're doing a reading while on a drug chemical high, wasted on alcohol, or if you've consumed a large meal or anything that could be considered a toxin to the body. This can make the reading come off all over the place and unclear.

Many professional psychics avoid reading for those close to them because they're not emotionally objective enough to give their best friend a clear reading. They will be gentler with the reading and attempt to read in a way that benefits the friend. Once you do that, then you've begun the process of contaminating the reading. The clearest readings are when the reader is centered, operating from a high vibration, focused, objective, and emotionally detached from the client.

It's common to read for oneself and bend the read to fit the answer you're hoping for. I've watched novices pull one card after another because they were unhappy with the card they were originally given. Once you do that you've corrupted the read and created a false reading that will not be based in truth. At that point you're just pointlessly throwing cards down.

One is not always objective with their own stuff and requires someone else that is emotionally detached from themselves in order to receive an unbiased reading. In those cases, you'll want to seek out a professional psychic reader that charges for their services. This is because the charge is an exchange of energy. You are giving them money in exchange for a product. In that movement there is a balanced reciprocated energy moving between you that gives a better reading. The more upset and emotionally distraught you are when giving a read, the more off and unclear the reading can be. Be clear minded, centered, and relaxed when giving a reading whether for yourself or another. This is another reason why readers generally do not give readings to those they know whether it is an acquaintance, friend, or family member. They may unknowingly alter the reading to positively favor their friend. This is doing an injustice because you're giving false hope.

Reading for a friend can also cause friction if the friend is not positively receptive about it or ends up criticizing the read. I've heard numerous cases and have close psychic medium friends that have said they watched friendships and connections end over a reading that was given. Some are uncomfortable when their friend is seeing challenging circumstances and stating it to them. I've certainly had this issue myself in the past, especially considering the way I communicate let alone read in general, which can be direct and bold.

Many professional readers, psychics, and mediums have been known to obtain readings from other professionals in their field for clarity.

I'm a believer that anyone can read better for themselves than anyone else when they are in a clear state of reception. I've gone to readers in the past and found that my own readings for myself were the ones that transpired and came to light. Because in the end who knows you better than you do! Even when I have read for myself, I'm not bending the read to suit me, but rather giving myself the cold hard truth. I have given myself readings in the past that were not pleasing, but ended up coming to fruition. I saw the messages in the reading as a warning to me, but also one that I knew was coming, but I just had to confirm it with the cards. This is also part of the reason I moved into the spiritual teaching work. It was to help others come to the answers on their own. Why go to someone to help you with something you can do on your own with your Spirit team.

I've watched others express disdain or unhappiness when they've pulled a Tarot card that appeared negative to them. Challenging is the more appropriate word. Everyone is challenged in their life. No one is exempt from that including the rich or famous. When you're challenged, then you grow and evolve. You also learn how to attract in what you desire. If a challenge is presented to you, then find ways to move through it. The Tarot reading is like any psychic reading in that it is giving you the probable forecast. This probable forecast is what is seen if things continue as they are, regardless if it's showing something positive or challenging. As a free will thinking soul you can alter that forecast to something else by your choices.

The Tarot can help as a guide in terms of offering suggestions of what's to come, but in the end every human soul has free will choice. If you make a choice that goes against what the Tarot presented, then you alter the read and wind up creating a new path to head down. This is beneficial if you are faced with challenging cards, which you objectively look at as areas where you need to make some changes. The Tarot can also give you a warning, which helps to pre-armor you with what's to come. I've certainly seen the end of a personal love relationship with the Tarot weeks before it took place.

The Tarot is not necessarily going to tell you what you need to do. It is up to you to decide that for yourself. When reading for others you want to avoid telling someone what to do. You don't want to interfere with another's free will. The ethics of an exceptional reader is to present what you're picking up on without judgment, but you cannot and should not make the ultimate decision for someone else. You simply say, "If you stay with this person, then this is what I see, but it's up to you on what you ultimately decide to do."

How to Conduct a Reading

Before conducting a reading, ensure you are in a centered, calm, and focused state of contentment. This will bring you the most accurate reading. If you're not in that state, then wait until you are. This is also why earlier in the book I offered practical tips on centering yourself and taking care of all parts of you. This way you can easily bring yourself to that state quickly rather than taking weeks. The way others read varies from one person to the next. Work on finding rituals or exercises to partake in that will assist in bringing you to that calm state.

One way can be to set up a personal altar or space you use for readings. If you don't have any space in your home, then designate one in a place that is uncluttered. This is where you are most comfortable and will be undisturbed during the reading. Whether that be on your bed, living room couch, or dining room table. Make sure there are no distractions when you choose to conduct a reading. You can turn this space into your own private temporary altar. You may choose to Sage the space before a reading to clear away all the negative energies. Create a calming sanctuary with candles burning, soft music playing, and incense burning. Lower the lighting a bit if you're able to.

Meditate for a few minutes or more before a reading until you are in a centered relaxed state. Take long deep breaths in and out as you relax, then say a prayer or personal invocation. Call in your Spirit team, God, your angels, guides, or whoever it is that you have a strong relationship with on the Other Side. When in doubt, call in your Spirit team to assist you with the card reading you're about to do.

While it's not always necessary to create all these bells, whistles, and theatrics, you will find your readings are clearer when you create the perfect environment within and without before conducting a reading. When you pose a question to the Tarot and find the response to be unclear, then re-word the question. Ask the question in a different way, then try again. If your questions are scattered, then the messages will be too.

Spreads

My soul is the core instrument I use to communicate with Heaven. It is a clear enough conduit that it's all I need before anything else. You have the same ability as well within you. I started to see spirits entering and leaving my room at the age of four. The spirit communication has been going on for as long as I can remember without letting up. When you've been doing something naturally for decades, then it's all you know. When I used to offer professional readings, I'd hold the deck in my hand answering the person's questions without consulting the cards. I need to be doing something with my hands, so this is when I'd start shuffling the deck, "Let's double check everything I've said."

One by one the cards would confirm it all. I adopted my own methods from an early age by using a personal rhythm that is nothing like the default set way that others have been trained to do when reading. I've never followed the norm or anyone else's formula, but rather throw cards down like a poker player in a fury. The instant message pops up a second after the card has hit the table.

I have also never used or worked with a Tarot spread in my life. I come to the information, messages, and guidance that is intended to come through without any obstacles and restrictions. I'm a Wise One that doesn't follow anyone else's set pattern or rules. Those that know me best know this to be true. This doesn't mean that this is the way to go. This is merely what works for me. If you are in the beginning stages of reading, then you may want to investigate if spreads are something you would be more comfortable using.

Those that have been super close to me for eons have all pointed out over the decades that they can tell when it's me communicating with them, or when it's a spirit from the higher realms coming through. They've pointed out a distinctly noticeable shift in the language and information that comes out of me that changes within a matter of seconds. It's as if they're having a conversation with numerous people!

As I'm posing the question to my Spirit team, I will hear through Clairaudience how many cards I'm being asked or guided to pull for the answer, and I stick with that. Trust how many cards you are guided to pull when you ask your question before you conduct a reading. Changing that number because you're unhappy with the cards that were revealed smears the reading. It ends up inaccurate and confusing. If you're unsure how many cards to pull, then stick with anywhere from 1-3 cards per question.

Tarot card readers interpret and read the cards in differing ways. Not all readers read cards in the same way. There is no right or wrong way, but however you're guided to read the cards. Some use spreads such as past, present, future spreads, or the Celtic Cross spread. While others use no spread, but pull the number of cards they're guided or asked to pull. A Tarot spread tells a story where each card emphasizes or gives new meaning to the cards that follow or surround it.

In a reading spread, the cards may either show something that already took place, is happening in your life now, or is coming up. It's up to you to determine where it falls in the time frame. If it's in the future or has not happened yet, then this is the probable future. It is foreseen that this is what is to come. Your future changes based on the decisions or indecisions you or others make based on free will. Therefore, it's equally important not to take a future forecast read too seriously.

Many professional readers tend to state that all reads should be taken with a grain of salt or used for entertainment purposes. They cannot be held liable or responsible for a read that did not come to fruition, or for influencing the person they're reading for to make a decision that ultimately causes heartache or additional challenges. This is another reason you avoid telling others what to do in a read. Not only does it interfere with their free will choice or life path, but it can also prompt the client to make a decision that makes things worse for them. You cannot put yourself in a position where you are held liable.

The cards show the trajectory of where a situation is headed. They can also offer guidance as to what changes you would need to make in order to bring something to fruition or to prevent a challenging circumstance from happening. You own your life and the direction you choose to allow it to go in. Be the master of your own ship.

The Tarot can intimidate some that feel they'll never be able to read. It is true that some people are better at it than others the same way that some people are better drivers. Even a beginner can dominate by hitting an accurate reading out of the gate. Don't worry so much about trying to be an efficient reader. The more you let go of the need to try to be, the easier it will get.

Because of my lifelong love for the Tarot, I ended up writing a Tarot guidebook called *Tarot Card Meanings*, which included the general messages of each card. This guide was specifically made for the novice that had trouble learning the basic meaning of a card. Readers would tell me that many of the Tarot books they would pick up were ripe with detail, but slim on the overall meanings of the cards. This caused confusion for some that messaged me if I knew what a card meant, so that's also what prompted me to devote a book solely about the meanings of each card and nothing else. There is nothing wrong with looking up the card meanings as you're learning, but you also don't want to base what a book says about a card as being verbatim, including my book. You most definitely don't want to conduct a professional reading for someone and then reach for a thesaurus in the middle of the reading.

Trying to learn the meanings of each card can be overwhelming, which was the reason I created a basic guide to help the beginners get their feet wet. The best way to read is to not stress out over trying to learn the descriptions of each card. Instead tune into your Spirit team's guidance and follow your gut as to the first hunch you get when you flip over a card when seeing it, rather than worrying about what a card means. You grasp what the overall energy and essence is about a card to help you get to the answer. One of the many benefits to using the Tarot is that it can also help sharpen your psychic senses, because you are called to use parts of your soul and spirit that you normally wouldn't be exercising in your everyday life. The Tarot helps you to use senses you normally ignore.

AFTERWORD

A Final Word

Spirit can hear your thoughts and feel your feelings. When you're wandering around talking to yourself out loud or in thought, then you are heard. When you are feeling down and frustrated, then you are felt. God and your Spirit team can hear your mind filled or mindless chatter as some might call it as well as when you're angry or feeling immense love. You may not be a believer in much, but whatever you're thinking Spirit can hear you. This is also why you cannot attempt to deceive God, since He and all heavenly beings know exactly what you're thinking, feeling, or up to. This is whether it's aligned with something Dark or Light, they are aware of it. This is also why those that try to get away with murder end up meeting their

Karma in some form, because you might think you got away with murder, but not with any heavenly being. The direction you aim your soul's energy is what will expand and bring more of that to you.

Spirit knows more about everyone on the planet than your own best friend or family members. You may feel misunderstood by those around you, but God and your Spirit don't misunderstand you. They know every shred of what you're experiencing or going through. They want to guide out of misery and towards enlightenment if you would pay attention to the feedback they give.

Many have admitted that when they've had a tough time in life that they've seen that glimmer of hope that is no doubt coming from Spirit. They could be driving around and then hear a song play or they see a billboard sign that just happens to have the exact words they needed to hear. It could be words that only someone they once loved used to say. It could be a psychic related tip that what they're desiring is coming and to stay hyper vigilant and focused in faith.

There is no special tried and true way to connect with Spirit. The more you take care of your body, mind, and soul on all levels, then the more psychic input you will pick up on. The less you stress, the more psychic communication you'll hear. The more centered you are, then the more psychic guidance you'll feel sifting through you.

When one thinks of psychic gifts, they get excited thinking that it's just about foretelling the future. This is the last thing on Spirit's list. They are about helping people fine-tune all aspects of themselves so that they can achieve and accomplish what they set out to do from their life purposes to making sounder decisions in life. They know the more you take care of you, then the happier you'll be. They want to see people happy and expressing love over joyless negativity.

The ultimate reason all souls have incarnated on Earth is to learn about love. The only way you can truly learn that is by being thrown onto a gigantic rock with people that are so different from you, it would take a miracle to get you to find that space of acceptance for them. This isn't to be confused with showering love on a terrorist, but learning to love also means learning to view life through the lens of the angels with emotional detachment. My higher soul's view is through this same lens of God, my Spirit Council, and Heaven's angels. We would rather see two people in love regardless of gender or belief, than someone residing in toxic negativity. When you've lost your way, revert to raising your faith and believing there is something greater than your problems. Move back into that glorious uplifting loving light of God's magnificent rays baptizing you in a blaze of optimism. This is the space that psychic communication is increased.

Acknowledgments

Thank you to God, my Spirit Team Council, and to all of the loyal readers that have hopped on this awesome train ride of mine and stayed on. I am forever blessed and grateful for your eternal support of the work we do. Thank you also for supporting the arts and the artists of the world.

ALSO BY KEVIN HUNTER

Stay Centered Psychic Warrior
Warrior of Light
Empowering Spirit Wisdom
Darkness of Ego
Realm of the Wise One
Transcending Utopia
Reaching for the Warrior Within
Spirit Guides and Angels
Soul Mates and Twin Flames
Raising Your Vibration
Divine Messages for Humanity
Connecting with the Archangels
Monsters and Angels
The Seven Deadly Sins
Love Party of One
Twin Flame Soul Connections
A Beginner's Guide to the Four Psychic Clair Senses
Tarot Card Meanings
Attracting in Abundance
Abundance Enlightenment
Living for the Weekend
Ignite Your Inner Life Force
Awaken Your Creative Spirit
The Essential Kevin Hunter Collection
Metaphysical Divine Wisdom (Series)

STAY CENTERED PSYCHIC WARRIOR
A Psychic Medium's Trip Through the Darkness and Light of the Spirit Worlds, and Other Paranormal Phenomena

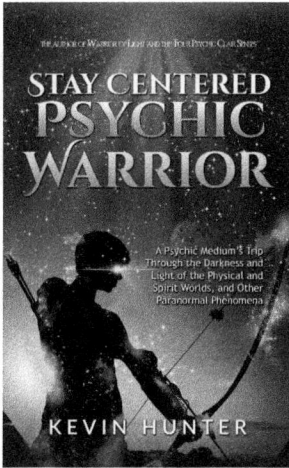

In *Stay Centered Psychic Warrior*, metaphysical teacher, psychic, medium, and author, Kevin Hunter talks about what it's like battling between mental health issues and the deeply potent psychic input that continuously falls into his soul's consciousness throughout each day. He offers plenty of examples and discussions of his brushes with spirit, seeing and hearing the dead, the power of the Darkness and the Light in both the physical and spirit worlds, along with sharing his numerous personal psychic and mediumship essays, glimpses of the Other Side, near death experiences, past lives, soul contracts, traveling to and from the Spirit Worlds, spirit guides and angels, recognizing your own psychic gifts, and much more!

This unique autobiography focuses on psychic and mediumship related content coupled with the soul's journey and purpose. Stay Centered Psychic Warrior is an intensely forceful and revealing read that doesn't shy away from the uncomfortable, the Darkness, abuse, mental health issues, while uplifting it with the many blessings of the Light and intriguing day to day psychic phenomena all in one. Allow it to inspire you to recognize your own psychic gifts knowing there is much more to this Earthly life than can be seen or comprehended. Be empowered to break through the rubble and stand strong and centered under the powerful Light that shines through any Darkness.

A Beginner's Guide to the
FOUR PSYCHIC CLAIR SENSES

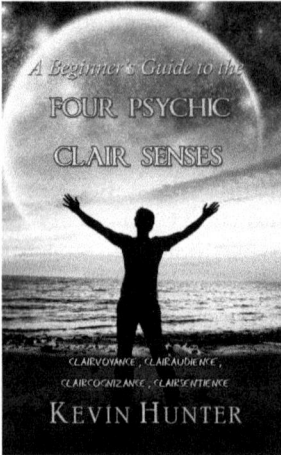

Many believe psychic gifts are bestowed upon select chosen ones, while others don't believe in the craft at all. The reality is every soul is born with heightened psychic gifts and capabilities, but somewhere along the way those senses have dimmed. All are capable of being a conduit with the other side, including those closed off and blocked to it. There are a variety of enlightened beings residing in the spirit realms to assist human souls that request their help. They use varying means and methods to communicate with you called clair channels. These clairs are crystal clear etheric senses used to communicate with any higher being, spirit guide, angel, departed loved one, archangel, and God.

The *Four Psychic Clair Senses* illustrates what the core senses are, examples of how the author picks up on messages, how you can recognize the guidance, and other fun metaphysical psychic stuff. You are a walking divination tool that allows you to communicate with Spirit. The clairs enable you to receive heavenly messages, guidance, and information that positively assist you or another along your Earthly journey. Read about the four core clairs in order to pinpoint what best describes you and how to have a better understanding of what they are and how they work for you.

TAROT CARD MEANINGS

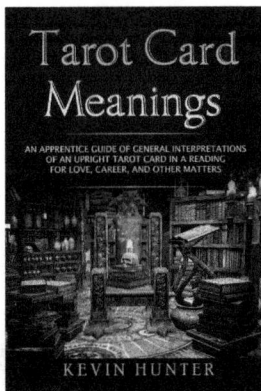

Tarot Card Meanings is an encyclopedia reference guide that takes the Tarot apprentice reader through each of the 78 Tarot Cards offering the potential general meanings and interpretations that could be applied when conducting a reading. The meanings included can be applied to most anything whether it be spiritual, love, general, or work-related questions.

Many novices struggle with reading the Tarot as they want to know what a card can mean in their readings. They grow stuck staring at three cards side by side and having no idea what it could be telling them. The Tarot Card Meanings book can assist by pointing you in the general direction of where to look. It will not give you the ultimate answers and should not be taken verbatim, as that is up to you as the reader to come to that conclusion. The more you practice, read, and study the Tarot, then the better you become.

Tarot Card Meanings avoids diving into the Tarot history, or card spreads and symbolism, but instead focuses solely on the potential meaning of a card in a general, love, or work reading. This gives you a structure to jump from, but it is up to you to take that energy and add the additional layers to your reading, while trusting your higher self, intuition, instincts and Spirit team's guidance and messages. Anything included in the Tarot Card Meanings book is an overview and not intended to be gospel. It is merely one suggested version of the potential meanings of each of the 78 Tarot cards in a reading. It may assist the novice that is having trouble interpreting cards for themselves.

ALSO AVAILABLE BY KEVIN HUNTER

Books that Empower, Enlighten, Educate, and Entertain!

Just as your body needs physical food to survive,
your soul needs spiritual food for well-being nourishment.

THE ESSENTIAL KEVIN HUNTER COLLECTION

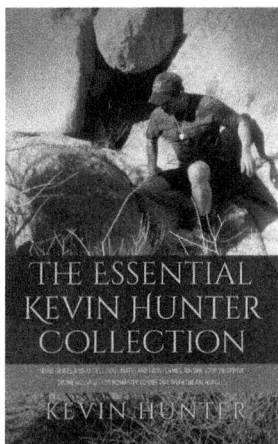

Kevin Hunter an empowering author specializing in a variety of genres, but he is most notably known for his work in the realms of spirituality, metaphysical, and self-help. He has assisted people around the world with standing in their power, and in having a stronger connection with Heaven, while navigating the materialistic practical world. Now some of his popular spiritually based books are available in this one gigantic volume.

The Essential Kevin Hunter Collection is the spiritual bible that contains over 500 pages of content geared towards improving and enhancing your life. It is for those who prefer everything in one gigantic book. The content included in this edition are from the books: *Spirit Guides and Angels, Soul Mates and Twin Flames, Raising Your Vibration, Divine Messages for Humanity, Connecting with the Archangels, Warrior of Light, Empowering Spirit Wisdom,* and *Darkness of Ego.*

THE ESSENTIAL
KEVIN HUNTER
COLLECTION

Featuring the following books
Warrior of Light, Empowering Spirit Wisdom, Darkness of Ego,
Spirit Guides and Angels, Soul Mates and Twin Flames, Raising
Your Vibration, Divine Messages for Humanity, and Connecting
with the Archangels.

TRANSCENDING UTOPIA
Reopening the Pathway to Divinity

Transcending Utopia is packed with practical and spirit knowledge that focuses on enhancing your life through empowering divinely guided spiritual related teachings, inspiration, wisdom, guidance, and messages. The way to accelerate existence on Earth towards Utopia is if every person on the planet resided in their soul's true nature, which is in a state of all love, joy, and peace. The ultimate Nirvana is surpassing that perfection through methods that a limited consciousness could ever dream possible. This is the exceptional glory your soul was born into before the dense turbulence of Earthly life enveloped and suffocated you.

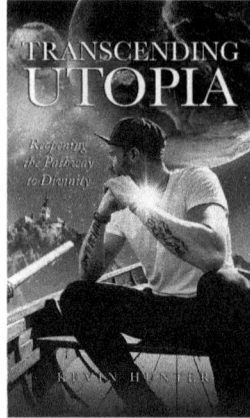

Transcending Utopia is to go beyond your limits and travel outside of the generic mundane materialistic achievement that human beings taught one another to thrive for. A utopian society is where everything is perfectly blissful on all levels according to the sanctified values you were born with. The sensations connected to how flawless everything feels in that moment reveals the authentic perfection you were made from. Utopia is the ideal paradise as imagined in one's dreams that seems to be inaccessible by human standards. It is a state of mind that is possible to reach by adopting broader ways of looking at circumstances while being disciplined about how you conduct your life. You search for a sign of this utopia through external means, only to be consistently left with disappointment. This is because utopia begins and ends inside the spark that burns within your spirit like a pilot light waiting to be ignited.

LIVING FOR THE WEEKEND
The Winding Road Towards Balancing
Career Work and Spiritual Life

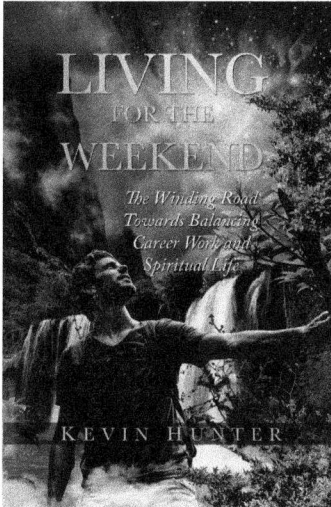

Working hard to ensure your bills are paid can leave your soul spiritually starved for soul nourishment. When your goal is to obtain enough money to be comfortable that you become carried away in that current, then there is little to no room for Divine enrichment.

Many work to survive in jobs they hate because it's the way it is. As a result, they experience and endure all sorts of emotional pain whether it is through depression, sadness, anger, or any other kind of negative stressor. Some silently suffer through this emotional strain gradually killing off their life force. If you don't have a healthy social life and positive fun filled activities and hobbies to balance that burden outside of that, then that could add additional tension. What's it all for if you can't live the life you've always wanted to live? Instead, you spend your days growing forever miserable and broken.

Living for the Weekend examines the pitfalls, struggles, as well as the benefits available in the current modern-day working world. This is followed up with spiritual and practical tips, guidance, messages, and discussions on ways to incorporate more balance and enlightenment to a cutthroat material driven world.

227

Attracting in Abundance
*Opening the Divine Gates to Inviting in Blessings and Prosperity
Through Body, Mind, and Soul Spirit*

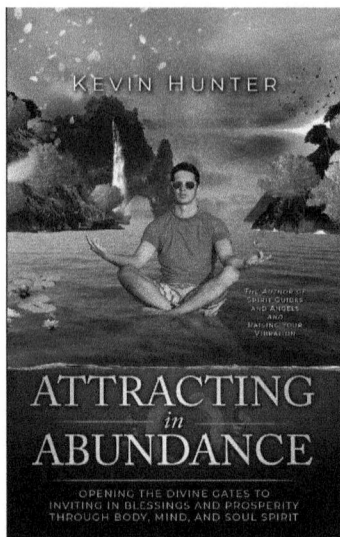

Having enough money to survive comfortably enough on this physical plane is part of obtaining abundance, but it's not the destination and purpose to thrive for. You could work hard to make enough money to the point you are set for life, but that won't necessarily equate to happiness. Achieving a content satisfied state of joy and serenity starts with examining your soul's state and overall well-being. When that's in place, then the rest will follow.

Attracting in Abundance combines practical and spirit wisdom surrounding the nature of abundance. This is something that most everyone can get on board with because all human beings desire physical comforts, blessings, and prosperity, regardless of their personal values and belief systems. *Attracting in Abundance* is broken up into three parts to help move you towards inviting abundance into your life on all levels. "Part One" contains some no-nonsense lectures surrounding the philosophies, concepts, and debates on the laws of attracting in abundance. "Part Two" is the largest of the sections geared towards fine tuning the soul into preparing for abundance. "Part Three" is the final lesson plan to help crack open the gates of abundance with various helpful tidbits, guidance, and messages as well as the blocks that can prevent abundance from coming in.

The B-Side to the Attracting in Abundance book

ABUNDANCE ENLIGHTENMENT
*An Easy Motivational Guide to
the Laws of Attracting in Abundance
and Transforming Your Soul*

Ultimate authentic success surrounds your soul's growth and evolving process. It's when you realize that none of the physical ego driven desires matter in the end. You can work hard to make sure you stay afloat, you're able to pay your bills, and support yourself and family, but you're not chasing popularity for external validation. Any amount of goodness displayed from your heart is the true measure of real accomplishment.

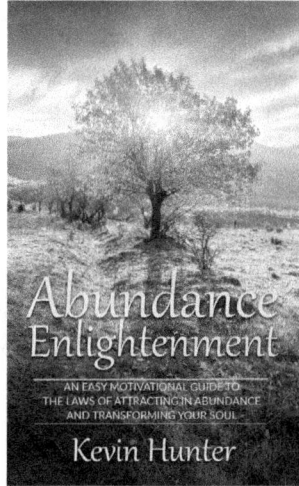

Abundance Enlightenment

AN EASY MOTIVATIONAL GUIDE TO
THE LAWS OF ATTRACTING IN ABUNDANCE
AND TRANSFORMING YOUR SOUL

Kevin Hunter

An overflowing feeling of optimism and love coupled with faith and action is what increases the chances of attracting good things and positive experiences to you. Abundance is more than monetary and financial increase. It can also be about reaching an optimistic well-being state of joy, peace, and love. This positive emotional mindful state simultaneously attracts in blessings.

Abundance Enlightenment is the follow up book to *Attracting in Abundance*. It contains both practical guidance and spirit wisdom that can be applied to everyday life. Some of the key topics surround the laws of attraction as well as healthier money management and improving your soul to help make you a fine tuned in abundance attractor.

MONSTERS AND ANGELS
An Empath's Guide to Finding Peace in a Technologically Driven
World Ripe with Toxic Monsters and Energy Draining Vampires

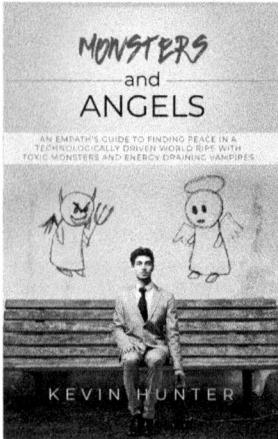

Every person on the planet is capable of being empathic and sensitive, to becoming an energy vampire or toxic monster. No one is exempt from displaying the darker sides of their ego. The easiest and most efficient way to spread any kind of energy is online. Every time you log onto the Internet, there is a larger chance you're going to see something related to the news, media, or gossip areas thrown in front of you, even if you attempt to avoid it as much as possible. You're absorbing everything that your consciousness faces, including the ugly and the wicked, which has its own consequences. This tempestuous energy is tossed into the Universe ultimately creating a flame-throwing battleground inside and around you.

Monsters and Angels discusses how technology, media, and social media have an immense power in distributing both positive and negative influences far and wide. This is about being mindful of what can negatively affect your state of being, and how to counter and avoid that when and wherever possible. Therefore, it's beneficial to govern yourself, your life, and your surroundings like a strict disciplined executive.

TWIN FLAME SOUL CONNECTIONS
Recognizing the Split Apart, the Truths and Myths of Twin Flames,
Soul Love Connections, Soul Mates, and Karmic Relationships

Twin Flames have a shared ongoing sentiment and quest from the moment they're a spark shooting out of God's love that explodes into a blinding white fire that breaks apart causing one to be two, until two become one again, separate and whole, and back around again. Looking into the eyes of your Twin Flame is like looking into the eyes of God, because to know love is to know God.

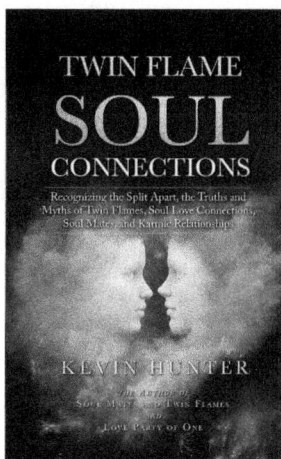

Twin Flame Soul Connections discusses and lists some of the various myths and truths surrounding the Twin Flames, and how to identify if you've met your Twin Flame, or if you know someone who has. The goal is not to find ones Twin Flame, but to awaken one's heart to love, and to work on becoming complete and whole as an individual soul through spiritual self-mastery, life lessons, growth, and raising your consciousness. Your soul's life was born out of love and will die right back into that love.

WARRIOR OF LIGHT
Messages from my Guides and Angels

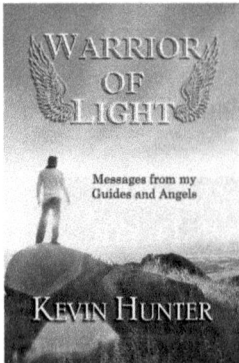

There are legions of angels, spirit guides, and departed loved ones in heaven that watch and guide you on your journey here on Earth. They are around to make your life easier and less stressful. Learn how you can recognize the guidance of your own Spirit team of guides and angels around you. Author, Kevin Hunter, relays heavenly guided messages about getting humanity, the world, and yourself into shape. He delivers the guidance passed onto him by his own Spirit team on how to fine tune your body, soul and raise your vibration. Doing this can help you gain hope and faith in your own life in order to start attracting in more abundance.

EMPOWERING SPIRIT WISDOM
A Warrior of Light's Guide on Love, Career and the Spirit World

Kevin Hunter relays heavenly, guided messages for everyday life concerns with his book, *Empowering Spirit Wisdom*. Some of the topics covered are your soul, spirit and the power of the light, laws of attraction, finding meaningful work, transforming your professional and personal life, navigating through the various stages of dating and love relationships, as well as other practical affirmations and messages from the Archangels. Kevin Hunter passes on the sensible wisdom given to him by his own Spirit team in this inspirational book.

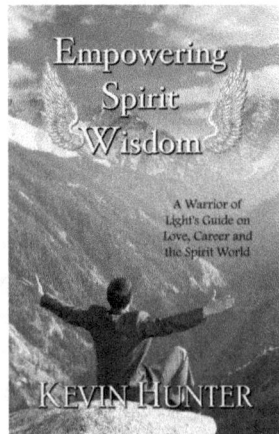

DARKNESS OF EGO

In *Darkness of Ego*, author Kevin Hunter infuses some of the guidance, messages, and wisdom he's received from his Spirit team surrounding all things ego related. The ego is one of the most damaging culprits in human life. Therefore, it is essential to understand the nature of the beast in order to navigate gracefully out of it when it spins out of control. Some of the topics covered in *Darkness of Ego* are humanity's destruction, mass hysteria, karmic debt, and the power of the mind, heaven's gate, the ego's war on love and relationships, and much more.

REACHING FOR THE WARRIOR WITHIN

Reaching for the Warrior Within is the author's personal story recounting a volatile childhood. This led him to a path of addictions, anxiety and overindulgence in alcohol, drugs, cigarettes and destructive relationships. As a survival mechanism, he split into many different "selves". He credits turning his life around, not by therapy, but by simultaneously paying attention to the messages he has been receiving from his Spirit team in Heaven since birth.

REALM OF THE WISE ONE

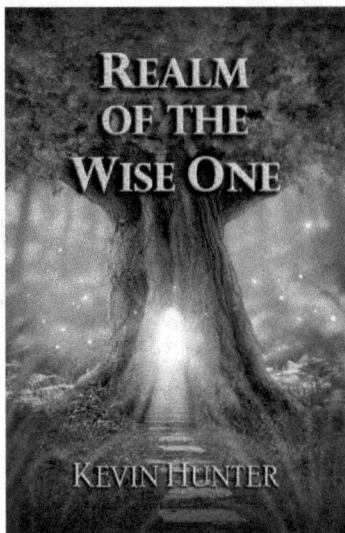

In the Spirit Worlds and the dimensions that exist, reside numerous kingdoms that house a plethora of Spirits that inhabit various forms. One of these tribes is called the Wise Ones, a darker breed in the spirit realm who often chooses to incarnate into a human body one lifetime after another for important purposes.

The *Realm of the Wise One* takes you on a magical journey to the spirit world where the Wise Ones dwell. This is followed with in-depth and detailed information on how to recognize a human soul who has incarnated from the Wise One Realm. Author, Kevin Hunter, is a Wise One who uses the knowledge passed onto him by his Spirit team of Guides and Angels to relay the wisdom surrounding all things Wise One. He discusses the traits, purposes, gifts, roles, and personalities among other things that make up someone who is a Wise One. Wise Ones have come in the guises of teachers, shaman, leaders, hunters, mediums, entertainers and others. *Realm of the Wise One* is an informational guide devoted to the tribe of the Wise Ones, both in human form and on the other side.

IGNITE YOUR INNER LIFE FORCE

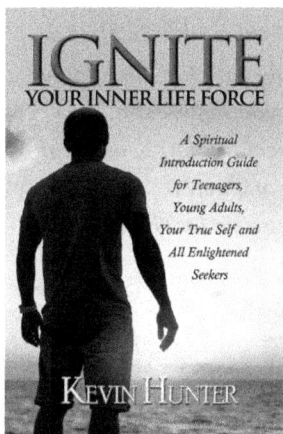

Ignite Your Inner Life Force is an introduction guide for teens, young adults, and anyone seeking answers, messages, and guidance and surrounding spiritual empowerment. This is from understanding what Heaven, the soul, and spiritual beings are to knowing when you are connecting with your Spirit team of Guides and Angels. Some of the topics covered are communicating with Heaven, working with your Spirit team, what your higher self is, your life purpose and soul contract, what the ego is, love and relationships, your vibration energy, shifting your consciousness and thinking for yourself even when you stand alone. This is an in-depth primer manual offering you foundation as you find a higher purpose navigating through your personal journey in today's modern-day practical world.

AWAKEN YOUR CREATIVE SPIRIT

Your creative spirit is more than being artistic and getting involved in creativity pursuits, although this is a good part of it. When your creative spirit is activated by a high vibration state of being, then this is the space you create from. You can apply this to your dealings in life, your creative and artistic pursuits, and to having a greater communication line with your Spirit team on the Other Side. *Awaken Your Creative Spirit* is an overview of what it means to have access to Divine assistance and how that plays a part in arousing the muse within you in order to bring your state of mind into a happier space.

THE *WARRIOR OF LIGHT* SERIES OF POCKET BOOKS

Spirit Guides and Angels, Soul Mates and Twin Flames, Raising Your Vibration, Connecting with the Archangels, Twin Flame Soul Connections, Attracting in Abundance, Monsters and Angels, The Four Psychic Clair Senses, The Seven Deadly Sins, Love Party of One, Abundance Enlightenment, and *Divine Messages for Humanity*

METAPHYSICAL DIVINE WISDOM
BOOK SERIES

On Psychic Spirit Team Heaven Communication
On Soul Consciousness and Purpose
On Increasing Prayer with Faith for an Abundant Life
On Balancing the Mind, Body, and Soul
On Manifesting Fearless Assertive Confidence
On Universal, Physical, Spiritual and Soul Love

♥

About Kevin Hunter

Kevin Hunter is the metaphysical author of dozens of spiritually based books that include *Warrior of Light, Transcending Utopia, Stay Centered Psychic Warrior, Metaphysical Divine Wisdom Series, Empowering Spirit Wisdom, Realm of the Wise One, Reaching for the Warrior Within, Darkness of Ego, Living for the Weekend, Ignite Your Inner Life Force, Awaken Your Creative Spirit,* and *Tarot Card Meanings.*

His pocket books include, *Spirit Guides and Angels, Soul Mates and Twin Flames, Raising Your Vibration, Divine Messages for Humanity, Connecting with the Archangels, The Seven Deadly Sins, Four Psychic Clair Senses, Monsters and Angels, Twin Flame Soul Connections, Attracting in Abundance, Love Party of One* and *Abundance Enlightenment.* His non-spiritual related works include the horror drama, *Paint the Silence,* and the modern-day love story, *Jagger's Revolution.*

Kevin started out in the entertainment business in 1996 as the personal development assistant guy to one of Hollywood's most respected acting talents, Michelle Pfeiffer, at her former boutique production company, Via Rosa Productions. She dissolved her company after several years and he made a move into coordinating film productions for the studios. His film credits include One Fine Day, A Thousand Acres, The Deep End of the Ocean, Crazy in Alabama, The Perfect Storm, Original Sin, Harry Potter & the Sorcerer's Stone, Dr. Dolittle 2, and Carolina. He considers himself a beach bum born and raised in Southern California. For more information and books visit: www.kevin-hunter.com

www.ingramcontent.com/pod-product-compliance
Lightning Source LLC
Chambersburg PA
CBHW060233050426
42448CB00009B/1421